TIME ZONES, BEER & LEFT-HANDED CHOPSTICKS

Your Travel Guide to Swing Kits, Used Appetizers, and the Toilet Tango

BRUCE BLANTON

PUBLISHED BY FIDELI PUBLISHING, INC.

© Copyright 2007, 2016, Bruce Blanton

THIRD EDITION

All Rights Reserved.

No part of this book may be reproduced, stored in a retrieval system, or transmitted by any means, electronic, mechanical, photocopying, recording, or otherwise, without written permission from the author.

ISBN: 978-1-60414-020-0

For information, please contact
Fideli Publishing, Inc.:
info@fidelipublishing.com

www.FideliPublishing.com

TABLE OF CONTENTS

Introduction .... *vii*

A Special Thank You .... *ix*

It Seems Normal to Me 1

Dining Out 15

Restrooms 33

Communication 41

Transportation 57

Lost Luggage 73

Hotels 79

Television 103

Air Travel 111

Cruising 137

Lasting Memories 151

Think About This… 165

About the Author 177

The cost of frequent travel is not always measured by the price of tickets. Time missed by being away from those we care for has a value in which a dollar amount cannot be assigned.

INTRODUCTION

My name is Bruce Blanton.

As an instructor in the semiconductor industry, I've had the pleasure of delivering training classes in 25 different countries. Throughout my career, I've circled the globe quite a few times and I have been fortunate enough to do it safely.

As I write this book, I think it is safe to say that I've probably seen more of the world in a year than many people will see in their lifetime.

This book includes details of my most memorable moments. I'm drawing on my experiences during 30-plus years of travel, and give you the perspective of life on the road through my eyes.

As a teacher, I've learned it's important to occasionally become the student and I sometimes allow human nature to be my instructor. I've had the pleasure of making friends all over the world, and I've also been involved in some unique learning experiences.

Have you ever wondered if dogs in Beijing bark in Chinese? If you answered this question with a yes, you probably have too much time on your hands, and you'll enjoy what you find on these pages. This book is also for the "Road Warrior." That person who lives from suitcases and considers meals delivered by room service as having a home cooked meal.

For those who rarely travel, this book will attempt to bring to life many of the things we take for granted in familiar surroundings and the comfort of our own homes.

If you are a frequent traveler, you'll probably recognize some of the situations described and possibly remember some of your own unique experiences.

A SPECIAL THANK YOU

I'd like to give a special thank-you to all the flight crews in the airline industry. They have made the toughest part of my travel (the long plane ride) pass quickly and painlessly. Over the last 30 years, I've spent a good deal of time away from home and I've always been treated with respect by these professionals, which makes the time away from home a little more bearable.

I'd also like to thank Saskia Jensen, my Travel Agent in Gilbert, Arizona. She has worked wonders when it comes to my last-second travel requests. There have been many opportunities when she could've left me stranded on some remote island — and I am sure that a couple of times she probably wanted to — but fortunately she has always managed to get me home to my family.

Bruce D. Blanton

IT SEEMS NORMAL TO ME

"…you see a family of four, their dog, an ironing board, and a birdcage all piled onto a motor scooter that passes you on the street…"

Many of my friends tell me how lucky I am because I get to travel. In one way, they're right. However, Dorothy in the *Wizard of Oz* said it best, "There's no place like home." Sometimes, learning to deal with different cultures can be confusing, complicated, or just downright strange.

What is Normal?

Traveling to another country where you don't speak the language can make going to a local restaurant a real experience. When the waiter brings you a bowl of a clear broth, you're careful to grab the correct spoon to try your "soup."

While you're trying to determine the flavor of this rather plain broth, you notice that every person in the restaurant is watching you. You think it's because you're the only American in an Asian restaurant. The truth is, they all know that you're eating from the finger bowl rather than washing your hands in it.

Or, you stop at a light in Korea and as you look out of your taxi window, you notice the front wheels of the small pickup truck beside you are off the ground. As the truck pulls away, you see ten full-grown pigs are staring at you from the truck bed.

And, in Taiwan you see a family of four, their dog, an ironing board, and a birdcage all piled onto a motor scooter that passes you on the street. Upon seeing this you may say to yourself, "I need to stop mixing cough syrup with my tequila poppers!"

I define "normal" as a behavior that's acceptable based upon where you are currently standing. What seems bizarre to some people in the U.S. is a way of life in other countries. Who am I to say that someone analyzing his or her earwax while conducting a conversation with you is strange?

The same goes for using the urinal at an airport in Japan while the cleaning lady is mopping between your feet and wiping the top of the urinal.

Then, there was the elderly lady in a Buddhist temple that farted at a sound level that would award her top honors and probably a trophy in almost any college frat house.

Normal has its good points, too. In Japan, you can walk down the street and find a vending machine that dispenses ice-cold beer!

I'm always amused when watching television in Asia and see dubbed versions of American TV shows. It takes a little time to get used to hearing Bugs Bunny speak with a deep male Japanese voice, or hear Pamela Anderson on *Baywatch* speaking with a voice two octaves higher than Minnie Mouse. Interestingly, I had to travel to Japan to realize *Baywatch* had dialogue.

One night I actually blew beer through my nose when I was channel surfing and came across John Wayne speaking Chinese to a woman. It was just so wrong (and funny) in so many ways.

Saturday in the Park

During one Saturday afternoon in Europe, I stopped at a lakeside pub to have a beer and get something to eat. I was talking to the gentleman doing the cooking on the barbecue. As I spoke with him, I thought it was really great to just have a normal meal on a Saturday afternoon in Europe. Then it hit me. What was normal about this? I was in Switzerland, eating German bratwurst cooked by a Jamaican from Kansas City.

Good Luck?

Once when entering a business in Taiwan, an employee pointed out to me that it's normal to have mini orange trees positioned by the door to bring the company good luck. It didn't take long for me to notice that their two good luck icons were almost dead. So I asked, "If they bring good luck, why are they dying?"

His reply was, "If they die, we just buy new ones."

I'm sure this makes sense to someone somewhere, so perhaps one day someone will be able to explain it to me.

What the Duck?

A coworker (Lee) and I were returning to our hotel in Beijing after that day's work. As we rode home in the taxi, I looked out the window and saw something odd. I took a second glance and then smiled real big.

Lee asked me why I was grinning, and I calmly said, "There's a man on the sidewalk walking a duck." As soon as I made the comment, a bus passed between the sidewalk and our taxi blocking the view. Lee tells me I've probably mistaken some ugly dog for a duck.

Just then, the bus pulled forward and we both looked over. We saw an elderly man walking with a duck on a leash. Now, here's where the story gets strange. On closer observation, the duck was wearing a red and black jacket with matching red boots.

We both knew that no description in the world would ever capture the true essence of what we saw. Furthermore, we were able to accurately predict the responses we would get from our friends after we told them about this "well dressed duck."

> *A side note to this story:*
>
> *During my flight home from this trip, I'd been discussing the development of this book with one of the flight attendants. About an hour before we landed, she came to my seat and said, "I have the cutest story for your book. At our hotel in Beijing, there was this man with a duck..."*

Sounds Like Trash to Me

In Taiwan, all of the garbage trucks play one particular song. The song announces that a garbage truck is in the vicinity and it's time to bring your trash to the curb for pickup.

The very first time I heard the tune, I thought it was an ice cream truck. Imagine the puzzled look on my face when I looked outside and realized that the music I heard was coming from a big yellow garbage truck. I can no longer see or hear an ice cream truck in the United States without thinking of Taiwan.

The song that's played on each of these "Mobile Trash Units" is Beethoven's "Fur Elise." I can only wonder why this song was selected out of all the possible tunes to represent garbage collection, especially when Country & Western music has so many more appropriate titles.

Imagine a child who's grown up in Taiwan and then moves to another country. At some point, they'll have to take a music appreciation class in school. When their teacher plays "Fur Elise" and asks for comments, the only natural response this kid will have is to associate this famous classical song with trash or garbage.

I'm going to go out on a limb here and guess that this won't be the response the teacher expects. While speaking only the truth, this student will be seen as a hero to his classmates and as a troublemaker by the teacher.

Some People's Children

I've traveled to many places and I will say without a doubt, if there is one place in the world where a "leash law" should be mandatory for children, it's Asia. For the most part, kids in Asia are nothing more than uncontrolled projectiles. You'll find them everywhere and they are always running at break-neck speed to get from point A to point B.

You'll find them in hotel elevators, on the stairs, and stuck in the revolving doors. More importantly, the place where I dread seeing them most is in restaurants. Here, they're no longer just projectiles, they're like projectiles on steroids. It's as if their parents wind them up and then turn them loose to inflict chaos on everyone in the vicinity.

I've also learned that if you are eating at a buffet where children are present, you'll find things in the pans that weren't there when the cooks delivered them.

The Hotel Dining Experience

On one trip, I was staying at a hotel in Korea. On a Sunday afternoon I decided I didn't want to go out and misinterpret any more menus, so I chose to have lunch in the hotel restaurant. As soon as I got to the hostess station, I noticed one long table that was packed full of children who were there to celebrate a birthday.

I started to rethink my decision, but then I noticed some business types huddled in a corner opposite the children so I asked to be seated near them. As I waited for someone to take my order, a little girl with a whistle came up behind me and let go with one of the loudest blasts I've ever heard. When I turned around with terror in my eyes and stared at her, she ran off and hid under the table near her parents.

I turned back around and tried to read the menu, while my eyes were still rattling back and forth from the brain-jarring whistle blast. A few minutes after that, a little boy came running out from behind a wall and plowed right into the stomach of a waitress who was carrying a tray of dishes. I know I was in Korea, but I definitely heard "China" crash.

Then, while I was eating my lunch, three boys showed up at my table and just stood there and stared at me while I ate. Wishing that I had a can of *Kid-be-Gone*, I stopped eating and just stared back at them. They started laughing and ran off.

All of this happened within a 30-minute period, and it seemed that my lunch had become one long nightmare. As much as I wanted to, I could not wake up.

As I waited for my bill in misery (misery is not one of the 50 states), my mind drifted off into bizzaro-world and I came up with this thought: *Euthanasia is the act of ending pain and suffering, which would mean that "Youth in Asia" is the act of inflicting pain and suffering.*

Welcome to Germany

After a nine-hour flight and a two-hour train ride, I arrived at my hotel in Freiburg, Germany. I took a quick nap and then decided to go downstairs to the hotel restaurant and get some food before going out to explore the city.

I sat down at the bar and asked for a menu. When I got it, I quickly realized I couldn't understand a single word that was written on it. I knew how to pronounce a couple of food items in German, like sauerkraut and Wiener schnitzel — so I looked intensely for those items.

As I was reading the menu, the bartender yelled at me rather loudly. I didn't understand what she said, so I just pointed my finger back at her and told her that I wasn't ready to order. Once again, she pointed at me and spoke even louder. I smiled at her and acknowledged her interest in my order.

A few seconds later, she grabbed the menu from my hands. It turned out that I was so intent on trying to find my secret words; I hadn't realized the candle in front of me was beginning to burn the plastic on my menu as I read it.

After nearly burning down the house on my first day in Germany, I went across the street to a little outdoor pub. As I sat there enjoying a beer, I noticed a peculiar noise off in the distance. It sounded like someone was shoveling rocks from a concrete surface.

The noise got louder and louder, then all of a sudden I saw a big flag with the Beck's Beer logo on it. It soon became obvious that the noise was coming from a German soccer team who were carrying their namesake flag as they paraded through the streets of Freiburg.

The loud noise I'd heard came from a man in the group who was wearing a white wedding dress. Part of his wedding dress ensemble included a "charm bracelet," made of heavy chain attached to his ankle. The charms attached to his anklet were various sized aluminum cans, which made a horrible sound with each step he took.

The funniest part of the whole event was watching the facial expressions of the people as they passed through the pub and saw the bearded man with the hairy back wearing a white wedding dress.

I found out later the man in the wedding dress was celebrating his bachelor party with his teammates.

Shrimp to Go

When I drive to work every morning, I usually see people doing things while they drive that just simply shouldn't be done while operating a vehicle. I've seen a man reading a newspaper or shaving. I've seen a woman putting on her makeup. It's common for me to pull up beside a person who's brushing his teeth as he drives.

I call these people crazy, but many people think this is normal. If this describes a normal driving experience in the U.S., then the following are the Asian equivalents I've observed while traveling.

In Korea, one day I was sitting in the back of a taxi on my way to work. I looked out the window to my right and saw a man with a bowl in his left hand, chopsticks in his right, and a jumbo prawn dangling from his mouth. He was steering his car with his knees while he used his chopsticks to dissect the prawn in his mouth. This was early in my travel experiences, and I hadn't quite mastered the fine art of using chopsticks. It was almost impossible for me to use chopsticks to pick up a prawn, even if I was sitting in a chair at a table and the prawn was tied to one of my chopsticks. Seeing this man doing this while driving was pretty amazing.

As we drove beside him, all I could do was stare and admire his dexterity. His eyes never once left the road, and he never swerved out of his lane. Of course it should be noted that during rush hour in Korea you can actually run out of gas on the freeway and not even know it until you exit. This is because the cars are packed so closely together and moving so slowly that you'd just get pushed along and not notice you were out of gas until you actually tried to leave the flow of traffic.

Bring Out the Big Guns

In the United States, we've become accustomed to seeing guns strapped to a policeman's hip and not much of anywhere else. In many other countries, though, it's quite normal to see guns carried in places where you least expect.

While in Manila, I went to a McDonald's and noticed two young security guards standing at the entrance, assault rifles in hand. Two things immediately became obvious. One, I probably had things in my refrigerator older than either of these "boys," and the other thing was their guns were so badly rusted and in such poor condition they probably couldn't fire if they tried to use them.

As you get on to some of the main roads in Israel, you'll see bus stops where many of Israel's military personnel wait for their rides. Every one of them has a rifle strapped to their shoulder as they stand, talk, or even kick a soccer ball during their wait.

I took a bus from my hotel in Korea to the airport. When we arrived at the airport entrance, the bus stopped and two soldiers got on carrying big guns. The two men stood in the front of the bus for about 2 minutes and looked at each passenger. Without a word or facial gesture, they got off the bus and we proceeded to the terminal.

The encounter, which took me totally by surprise, was in 1998 at the Tel Aviv Airport as we entered the security checkpoint. It was about 9 p.m. when we pulled up to the entrance. My taxi driver rolled down his window and immediately the airport security officer pointed the business end of a machine gun at me. The barrel stopped about 12 inches from my face. Then, a second officer tapped on the passenger side window and asked to see my tickets and passport.

Knowing that my passport photo already made me look like a terrorist, I put on the biggest fake smile I could and handed him my passport, all the while staring at the gun. This event must've shaken me up more than I realized, because it took me nearly an hour to get that silly smirk off my face.

Telling It Like It Is

When it comes to matters of a person's weight, Americans either politely avoid the issue or wait until the person leaves the room so that negative comments can be made behind the person's back. Every time I return to Asia, I'm usually greeted with, "Bruce, it's good to see you," followed by "You're much fatter now."

As I age, my muscles have decided to start relocating closer to my stomach. At six feet tall and 225 pounds, I don't consider myself fat. After not seeing someone for six months, being greeted with, "You're much fatter now," feels about the same as taking a knee to the groin.

In Singapore, our sales representative always drives us to and from our appointments. After I'd been there a couple of days on my most recent trip, I once again got "that fat pain" when I found out the sales manager, Bryan, had instructed one of his employees to rent a larger car so that his personal car wouldn't tilt to one side when I rode with him. I've never to my knowledge caused a car to tilt and I was pretty much offended by this logic.

I know there've been bigger and taller people than me who've visited Asia; it just seems I'm trapped in the same horrible nightmare every time I return to teach a class. For example, when I teach at many locations, I'm required to wear clean room garments (a.k.a. Bunny suits). I'm also required to put on special footwear, such as slippers or clean room boots.

I wear a size 12 shoe, but it seems all footwear in Asia stops at size seven or eight. Small boots are just plain uncomfortable and small slippers don't stay on my feet. It's hard to gain any respect from my students when I walk down the hall and launch my slippers five feet in front of me or send them to the bottom of a stairwell.

In Taiwan, it took them about an hour to find a Bunny suit that would fit me. Once they found it, they marked it so everyone knew it was mine and nobody else was to touch it. The special identifying marking was a one-foot wide sticker with the word "Jumbo" written on it.

"Jumbo" and his friends

DINING OUT

"...this is the best pickled crow gizzard I've ever eaten."

When traveling throughout Asia it's normal to see a display case filled with examples of the food served in the dining establishment you are about to enter.

For me, there's nothing like seeing a lacquered plastic omelet (that's been sitting in the sun since plastic was invented), to really get my digestive juices flowing. Unfortunately, these display cases can't prepare you for the taste of what you are about to eat.

As a traveler and guest in many countries, I'm often taken out to dinner. I've learned over the years not to ask what my hosts have ordered. I just eat it. Most of the time the food tastes great, and there's no reason to worry.

However, occasionally you'll bite into something that provides a certain taste you weren't expecting. For a brief moment, the food is trapped in your mouth while your brain is trying to analyze it. Your taste buds have already reached their conclusion and your instinct is to spit it across the room. Thankfully, no matter how hard you try, for

In Singapore with beer, spicy noodles, and barbequed stingray; it doesn't get any better than this.

some reason your mouth just won't open and you save yourself the embarrassment of spitting.

Meanwhile, your host is watching you, eagerly awaiting your approval of the delicacy he's ordered for you. All this time the food is going up and down in your throat like an out of control elevator. You start to panic, but know you must show composure so your host isn't offended. So you force yourself to smile appreciatively.

Finally, one of two things happens, you eventually swallow and say, "This is the best pickled crow gizzard I've ever eaten," or you reach for a glass of water to wash it down only to end up with half of what you had in your mouth floating in your glass.

Most restaurants in Japan provide special tables where you remove your shoes and sit cross-legged on a wooden floor for what seems like weeks if you're not used to sitting this way. When it's time to leave, you find your legs have fallen asleep and you have absolutely no control over the direction you'll be moving. Unless you find a wall to prop yourself up against until the feeling comes back, you usually end up as an unwanted guest at the table behind you.

This type of seating style creates its own special atmosphere. Where else can a group of men go after a hard day's work and have six pairs of sweaty feet just inches from their dinner plate. I'm willing to bet that's where the phrase "Odor Eaters" originated.

Many foreign restaurants have pictures on the menu showing you the food they serve. Unfortunately, from time to time you'll encounter a restaurant where the menus have no pictures. As if that weren't bad enough, the menu's also written in a language you can't read.

At this point, you have to make a decision: (1) Get up, put your shoes back on, and leave the restaurant while everyone smiles at you because you looked out of place and this only confirms their thoughts. Or (2) play what I call "Menu Roulette." This is where you point at something on the menu and just pray you're not ordering the pickled crow gizzard again. This option, however, may create confusion for your waiter if you point to something like, "Kids under 12 eat for free."

In Ireland, a work associate, Tom, and I would many times walk into a totally empty restaurant expecting to get served fairly quickly. To our surprise, we'd be asked if we had a reservation. After saying no, the hostess would roll her eyes and say, "Let me see if something is available."

We could see the only thing happening in this restaurant was the passing of time. However, the hostess would still walk around to determine the best place to seat us. Then, she'd tell us that she needed the table back in "three hour's time." We decided this statement had something to do with St. Patrick's Day, somehow.

Speaking of St. Patrick's Day. Tom and I witnessed a group of guys eating in a restaurant on St. Patrick's Day. One of the guys fell sound asleep at the table; he'd probably drunk his weight in Guinness Beer. His good friends got up and left him there, asleep at the table.

The waiter came over after they left and tried just about everything he could do to give the snoozing guy the bill. Once the man started snoring, we watched the waiter, who knew it was a lost cause at this point, stuff the bill into the sleeping man's shirt pocket and walk away.

Where's My Dinner?

My very first trip outside the United States was to the Philippines. Needless to say, it was also my first experience when it came to ordering food in another country.

On my first night, I decided I wouldn't be too adventurous and opted to go to the hotel restaurant. After figuring out the menu, I ordered a plate of spicy noodles. The dish came fairly quickly, but there was hardly anything to it. So, I called the waiter over and ordered

No waitress shortage in Singapore

some spicy chicken. Once again, the amount of chicken brought to me was barely enough to fit in the palm of my hand. So one more time, I ordered a plate of vegetables, which also came as a small portion. The whole process took about an hour and a half and earned me the amount of food that could have come on one plate.

Day two came and I decided to go back to the same restaurant. This time, I made an attempt to speed things up so that I could get served in less than an hour. My plan was to simply order the same three dishes I'd had the previous night, but this time I'd order them all at the same time.

I sat for a while. People came, ate their meal and left. I had no food. More people came, ate, and left. I was growing old sitting there, and still no food.

Finally, I stopped my waiter and asked where my meal was. He replied that I'd ordered three dinners and they were waiting for the other two people to arrive. When I told him that all three meals were for me, he was amazed.

He made sure the entire staff knew I was a "big" eater and they brought me extra rolls. Then, when other people were done eating, any food that was left behind was also brought by my table to see if I wanted it, too.

How Big is Small?

While in Singapore we went to a nearby island called Sentosa. After a day of sightseeing, four of us decided to go to one of the resorts for dinner. We decided on a restaurant in a beautiful hotel that featured viewing the spectacular sunset while eating dinner.

As we looked at the menu, we noticed each dish required you to choose between small and medium. Two of us were frequent travelers to Asia and knew there was no such thing as large here. We also knew that medium meant small by American standards. The only real decision was figuring out how many mediums of each dish we should order.

We asked our waitress if a medium dish was enough for two people, and she told us it was. What she should've said was the medium portion would feed two people plus the entire Green Bay Packer's offensive line.

When our order was ready, it took three people carrying massive trays to get our meals to our table. At one point, our waitress actually asked us if we wanted to move to a bigger table because there were so many dishes of food.

We ate for what seemed like hours and it still looked like we'd never started eating. Our waitress returned and asked if we wanted dessert. Immediately the ladies at our table said yes, then reality took control. We ended up leaving most of our meal at the table and I'm willing to bet the hotel staff had quite a feast after we left.

Pizza in the Philippines

After a couple of weeks in the Philippines, my boss, John, and I were kind of tired of eating the local food and decided we needed some American food. There was a pizza restaurant next to the hotel, so what we'd be eating was a "no-brainer."

We walked into the restaurant and the place was packed. The hostess approached us and asked if we wanted to be seated in a booth. We told her yes, and almost immediately she came back and was ready to seat us. We actually thought we were getting some sort of special treatment.

She took us to our booth and being the observant people that we were, we quickly noticed there were people already seated there. On one side were two adults and two small children who were halfway through with their meal. John and I sat down with them, thinking it was strange, but when in Rome…

We said hello and the only response we got was from one of the children who said, "American Joe." He then continued to say it about 20 more times. The family of four was sharing a small pizza.

John and I each ordered a large pizza and a pitcher of beer. When our order arrived, the family suddenly seemed to turn into an oil painting. They didn't move, they just sat and stared at us. We ate; they stared. We drank; they stared.

When the waitress delivered the family's bill, John and I thought it would be a nice gesture for us to pay it; so we did. This act of kindness opened the floodgates of conversation. They started with thank you and didn't stop talking to us for the next 30 minutes. Apparently they'd initially been afraid of the "scary Americans."

Sounds "Corny" to Me

It doesn't matter which Asian country you're in, they all have one thing in common — CORN. If you order a salad, you get corn on it. If you order a pizza, it comes with corn. Soup has massive amounts of corn in it. You can order fish and find that the eyes have been surgically removed and replaced with kernels of corn.

You can travel from one end of Japan to the other and see a bazillion rice fields, but nowhere will you find a cornfield. However, as soon as you order food, corn will magically appear out of nowhere!

You'll find corn on or in things that just don't seem right, too. It's in your bread, in your rice, in your waiter's hair, stuck to the back of your taxi seat, and you'll also find that it's the Flavor of the Month at the local ice cream parlor.

However, if you try to order a bowl of corn as a side dish, you're given a look like you've just grown a third eye. Corn is something you add to a dish to enhance the flavor, you don't eat it by itself. It would be like going into a restaurant in the United States and ordering a steak, potato, and a bowl of croutons.

I Don't Feel So Good

After traveling all over the world (and Texas), you'd think I'd know how to pack for the climate conditions of the country where I'll be traveling. Well, not always...

One December, I had a one-week stay in Japan. The purpose of the trip was to give three days of presentations at a semiconductor show. Instead of bringing heavy coats and rain gear, I brought Polo shirts and a light sweater.

From the time I arrived in Japan, it either rained or snowed and the temperature stayed right around zero degrees Celsius. At the end of the first day of the show, I started feeling ill. By early the next morning, I had a runny nose, a slight fever, and I was coughing up something that wasn't real pretty. It was obvious I wasn't going anywhere that day, so I decided to spend day two of the show in bed at the hotel.

I slept most of the day except for the times when I was awakened by phone calls from housekeeping. They kept calling my room because I had the "Do Not Disturb" sign on my door all day and they wanted to clean my room. Around 6 p.m. that evening, I got out of bed and felt great. I showered and called my coworkers to see what they were doing for dinner. They told me where they were going and I decided to meet them at the restaurant.

Once I got to the restaurant, I sat down and was immediately greeted with a plate of raw oysters. Normally raw oysters are not a problem for me, but on this particular day, I had to give them a second thought. Now, I'm expected to eat something in those shells that looks exactly like what I had been coughing up all morning.

Not wanting to be a "party-pooper," I figured I'd go for it and eat the oysters. I believe the oysters had some sort of magical powers because I'd swallow the oysters and a second later they were back in my mouth. I'd swallow them again and before I knew it, they were back. After a few minutes of this, I realized that I had an audience. Everyone at my table was watching me struggle with the oysters.

Finally, I gave up and unloaded what was in my mouth into a nearby napkin. I thought the worst was over, then two new plates arrived. One was filled with pickled chicken's feet and the other was "chicken knuckles" (the ends of the drumsticks that are deep fried.)

I sat there for a few seconds, then realized that perhaps I was not as well as I thought.

After 15 minutes, I couldn't come up with any justification as to why I should put pickled chicken's feet into my mouth. I eventually decided to go back to the hotel, where I ordered some fried noodles from room service.

The Toothpick

In Asia, you can stick your finger in just about any orifice and analyze whatever comes out while you're in public, and that's okay. However, if you forget to cover your mouth while picking your teeth, you'll end up with your picture on a poster at the local post office. There's a rule in Asia that you must cover your mouth when you use a toothpick.

Leftovers

In Taiwan there is an excellent restaurant that Lee, a coworker, and I always go to because it's close to our office. It took us a couple of visits, though, before we got used to seeing people sitting at their tables along with the family pet. The service and food has always been good and as long as I don't hear barking coming from the kitchen, I'm totally happy to eat there.

One evening at one of our favorite restaurants in Taiwan, Lee and I started ordering dishes as we always do. Usually within minutes, our orders are brought out to us one dish at a time. Early into our meal, we received one meat dish that neither of us had ordered. We figured we probably mispronounced something, being that neither one of us could actually read the menu, and we'd got this instead of something we expected.

We both ate from the dish, since in Asia it's common for everyone to pick from the same plate. We found the plate of unidentified meat to be quite tasty.

About 10 minutes after our dish of mystery meat arrived, our waitress walked by and without breaking stride or saying a word, picked up the plate and swiftly placed it in front of the people sitting three tables away from us.

Apparently, our waitress had accidentally given us someone else's order. Instead of telling us what happened, she just took the partially eaten meal from our table and gave it to its rightful owner.

Used Appetizers?

Lee and I ordered some appetizers at a rather popular pub in Taiwan. After about 45 minutes, our order was nowhere to be found. Finally, they brought us something we didn't order and didn't want. We told the waitress that what she delivered was incorrect and to just cancel our order.

The cancellation request seemed to upset her and she argued a bit, but we knew they hadn't started to cook the correct item. Reluctantly, she agreed to cancel our order. Meanwhile, the basket of deep-fried something just sat there next to us and the staff nibbled from the basket for the next 20 minutes.

Later on, our waitress returned to us and made a serious offer that still has Lee and me laughing to this day. While she was holding the half-full basket of unwanted, cold, unidentifiable fried objects that had been touched by ten different people, she told us that she'd make us a special deal and let us have the remainder of the basket for half price.

The Avocado Milkshake

On one trip to the Philippines, I decided to have lunch in the company cafeteria at the site where I was teaching. I sat down with some of my students and noticed three of the ladies had what looked like green milkshakes. I asked what they were drinking, and they told me it was avocado milkshakes.

Immediately I asked for a repeat. They couldn't have said *avocado* milkshakes. They confirmed that was exactly what they'd said. I said something original like, "Yuck!"

I told them I'd never heard of an avocado milkshake. Then they asked me how I "take my avocados." I replied that I usually ate them sliced up on a sandwich. They too replied with something original like the native equivalent of, "Yuck!"

This was too irresistible for me. I had to try one, so I ordered my first avocado milkshake. It was very good and it impressed me.

The next day, one of the ladies came in and told me she went home, sliced an avocado and put it on some bread. When she tried to eat it, though, she said she couldn't. "It just didn't seem right!"

Authentic Sushi

It's totally normal to go to a popular sushi restaurant in Portland, Oregon and be greeted by the manager, who is a very polite Asian gentleman. Then, a pretty Asian hostess dressed in a kimono will walk you through the restaurant that's decorated with all sorts of Japanese paraphernalia. She'll guide you to the sushi kitchen, seat you at the sushi bar and promptly get you a bottle of Sapporo beer and some sake. Then, Rafael and José will prepare your authentic Japanese meal.

All You Can't Eat

I'd been a guest for two weeks at a nice business hotel in Seoul, Korea. Every morning of my stay I'd go through the same breakfast routine. I'd sit down, the waiter would come over and I'd ask for coffee, then I'd tell him I wanted the buffet for breakfast. I'd eat, pay my bill, and go to work. This took place without incident for 12 consecutive days.

Then day 13 arrived. The "me and the waiter" interaction took place just like clockwork. I walked up to the buffet table and as I opened each of the eight warming pans, I noticed they had all been picked clean. There wasn't even any food to scrape off of the sides of the pans. I got some toast and some orange juice, sat down, and waited for them to bring out more food.

Ten minutes passed and nothing came out from the kitchen. Twenty minutes passed and still no food. After a half hour, it was time for me to leave for work. I walked up to the cashier and said that I only had coffee, toast and one glass of juice. I figured she'd be able to total up the individual items and charge me. But no, she hits me with 16,000 Won, which is about $20 US dollars. I repeated that I only had coffee, toast and one glass of juice. She said, "No, you ordered buffet."

I replied that there was no food at the buffet table. She then pointed to where the buffet tables were and said, "There is buffet." I saw this was going nowhere quick, so I asked for the manager.

The manager came over to the cashier, and she explained her version of the situation to him. The manager looked at my bill and walked over to my waiter was standing. The two of them talked for a moment and the manager returned. He hands me the bill and says, "You ordered buffet."

What was once amusement was now becoming anger. I asked the manager to follow me. We went to the buffet table and as I opened every one of the eight warming pans, I pointed out that each one was EMPTY!

He reopened the first three pans, stops, looks at me and says, "No food!" I agreed with his brilliant deduction. He apologized for the confusion and agreed to charge me for just the coffee, toast and one glass of juice.

The "Asian" Hotel Buffet

I travel a lot and I've had countless numbers of hotel meals, many of which included the breakfast buffet. In American hotels, people usually trickle into the dining area one or two at a time. They grab their food and sit down with very little commotion.

In Asia, I occasionally stay in large hotels that are frequent stops for tour groups. There are two rules that all Asian tour groups strictly enforce: (1) Always be on time for the bus. (2) Attack the breakfast buffet and take no prisoners.

It didn't take me long to learn that if I wanted to eat breakfast, I had to be in the dining area before 7 a.m. or I'd be caught up in one of the ugliest feeding frenzies ever seen. Here's an example: I was eating my breakfast in an almost empty dining area at one of the largest hotels in Kaohsuing, located in southern Taiwan. Out of nowhere came a "swarm" of Asian senior citizens blasting their way through the entrance and into the dining area. They entered with so much force it almost seemed to suck the air out of the building.

In a matter of minutes, a seemingly desolate restaurant was transformed into total chaos. It didn't take long before there were four people sitting with me who hadn't been there a couple of minutes prior.

Busloads of people fanned out as if they were assigned to go to various areas of the restaurant and report back on what type of food was in their corner of the building. They would descend upon their assigned area, remove all food that was present, and then bring the food back to their tables where "mini buffets" were created. This maneuver was so well choreographed that it almost seemed like I was eating with the Taiwan Olympic Buffet Team.

Did I Really See That?

Sometimes when you travel, you'll see some things that make you do a double take. Many people take the role of restaurant food inspectors in the U.S. for granted, but they shouldn't. After sitting down and just observing, here are some things that I've seen in other countries:

- A bartender clipping his fingernails while standing behind the bar.
- A sushi chef wiping sweat from his forehead with a towel, then wiping a knife with the same towel and cutting fish with that knife.
- After eating from a bowl of peanuts at a bar, the conversation comes to an abrupt stop when a roach crawls out of the bowl.
- A waiter flossing his teeth at the bar as he is talking to a cook.
- In a grocery store, a mother has her young son pee in the corner behind some boxes of fruit.
- Moving an object on a table and seeing three bugs run out from underneath it.
- A customer trying to chase bugs from a sushi display case with his cigarette lighter.
- A cook tasting sauce from a ladle and then putting the ladle back into the sauce.

- At a Thai restaurant, ants floating in every glass of water brought to our table.

Don't Expect What You Expect

When dining in restaurants outside the United States, never take anything for granted. Just because you're used to a certain service, do not assume the country you're in provides that same service. I learned this the hard way during my first international trip to the Philippines.

While at a restaurant waiting for a friend to show up and join me for lunch, I had a couple of appetizers and some iced tea as I waited. My friend ended up being unable to join me, so I went ahead and ordered my meal and just continued to get refills on my tea.

When I was done and ready to leave, I was given my bill and I almost hit the floor. It turns out that refills of iced tea are not free at this restaurant. I'm guessing that I had six or seven refills during the hour I sat at my table. When I looked at my bill, my tea was nearly double the cost of my food order.

Not to long after the "Ice Tea Incident," I was in Singapore with a coworker at a waterfront restaurant. We were there to try the chili prawns we'd been hearing so much about. We'd also been told the prawns were quite messy to eat.

We ordered our prawns and sat down. When our massive platter of prawns arrived, we couldn't help but notice the amount of chili sauce covering them, but figured we'd be up for the challenge.

After the waiter set the platter down, he handed us a plate and one paper napkin each. After only a few seconds, our napkins were no longer useful to us. I flagged down our waiter and asked for more napkins. He asked us how many we'd like. We both thought this was an odd question, but I picked a number and asked for five. The waiter

Jumbo prawns at Newton's Circus in Singapore

then informed us there was a charge for extra napkins (about ten cents per napkin).

It wasn't that we couldn't afford the 50 cents for the napkins, it was the principle of the matter — we weren't going to let anyone take advantage of us. So to make our point, we declined the napkins — a decision we would soon regret.

We ended up with chili sauce everywhere. It was in our eyes, in our hair, on our clothes and probably all over the taxi that took us back to the hotel. As I write this book, I think I'm still finding chili sauce several years later.

When we got to work the next day, we saw the person who recommended that particular restaurant, and before we could say a word he told us it was advisable to take napkins with you when you go there to eat.

RESTROOMS

"... I went from being on top of the world to wishing I'd taken notes during potty training."

The Asian Toilet

I'm in a foreign country, I have many people taking me to dinner, I'm eating different foods, I'm on an expense account, I'm invincible... That's what I thought, anyway.

One evening in Japan, we were eating a nice, classy dinner when all of a sudden, nature called. This was a call that couldn't be put on hold. I excused myself and went into the men's room. On the walk down the hallway I was actually thinking that I was really lucky to be there.

All of that thinking came to an abrupt halt as soon as I opened the stall door for the toilet. I stood there for about a minute contemplating this new turn of events. There was no toilet like the ones I was used to in the U.S. Instead, there was a hole in the floor lined with porcelain.

Suddenly, I went from being on top of the world to wishing I'd taken notes during "potty training." *Okay,* I thought, *it's just like going*

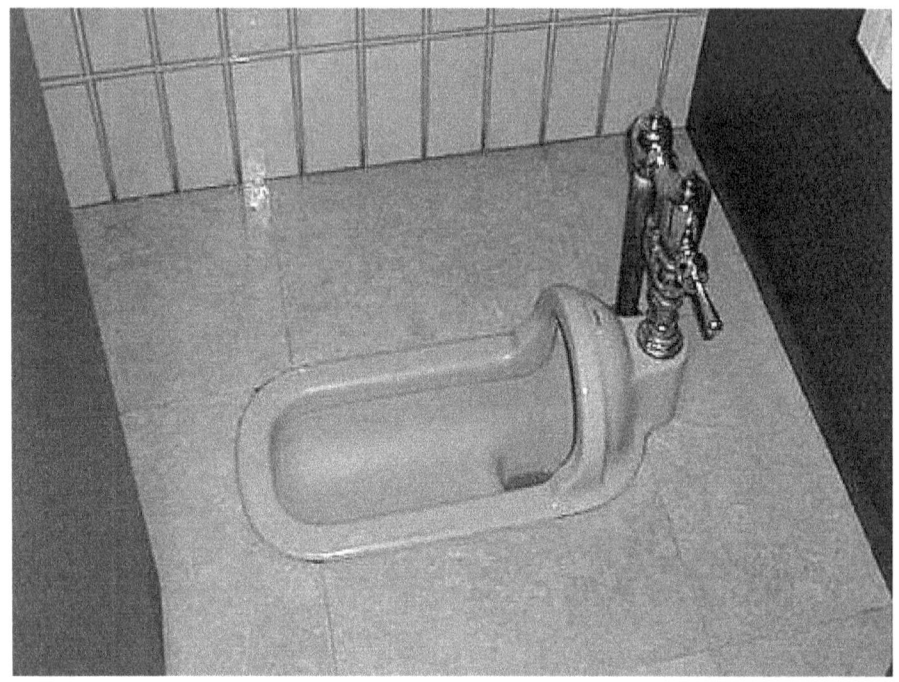

in the woods, but without the bugs. The only thing is, I've never had to go in the woods. Oh, it can't be that hard...

Then another thought came to mind. I'd been drinking most of the night. Now I had to squat and maintain my balance while performing a bodily function. To make matters worse, I realized that if you're not positioned correctly, you could do some serious damage to your pants. I didn't bring spare pants into the men's room with me, so I did the logical thing and removed my pants.

I'm 40 years old and all of a sudden something that has been natural for me for so many years has suddenly become a big ordeal. I finally completed my mission and felt like I deserved a medal or something. When I returned to the table, everyone asked why I was gone so long. I just looked at my host and said that I went camping. To this day, I refer to using an Asian toilet as "camping."

About a month later, I was traveling with a coworker and he had to go "camping." He'd never used an Asian toilet, but he knew what to expect. In this restaurant, though, there was an added twist — the toilets didn't have doors on the stalls. When he returned, he, too, was proud of his accomplishment.

He mentioned that his only issue with the experience was that when people walked into the restroom where he was taking care of business, they all looked at him as he squatted. He said he just acknowledged their presence with a head nod as they as they walked by him.

He also mentioned that while squatting, the toilet paper was directly behind him, which he thought was an awkward location. At that point, a big grin covered my face — he'd used the toilet facing backwards!

When "Going" Gets Tough

When in Taiwan, my job usually requires that I visit customers at both ends of the island. Doing this means I must spend 5 hours on a bus to get from one location to the other. There are two major factors that make this ride extremely uncomfortable. The first is that the highway between the two cities is in horrible condition, with potholes everywhere. The second is that it seems none of the buses have adequate shock absorbers.

After several years of traveling to Taiwan, the day finally came when I was forced to use the restroom on the bus. On these cross-country busses, the passengers ride upstairs while the driver, luggage, and the restroom are located downstairs.

The door to the restroom is four feet high. Once inside, the headroom really opens up — to a massive five feet. The thing is, I'm six feet tall. The restroom normally has the square footage of your average phone booth. So, by comparison, an airplane bathroom is enormous.

Once inside, the first thing I noticed was I had to deal with another one of those Asian toilets. I was just glad that what I had to do could be accomplished standing up.

I'm certain the bus drivers must lead a lonely life, because the only time they get any entertainment is when a passenger goes into the restroom. Once a passenger enters, the driver seeks out every possible pothole in the road and hits all of them, causing the person in the restroom to bounce around all over the place.

You can't use both hands on the walls to brace yourself because you need one hand to hold "things" in place. One hand on the wall serves no purpose in this situation.

I quickly learned there was a benefit to the limited head space. I ended up pushing my head against the ceiling to wedge myself in place. With both of my feet pressed firmly against each wall, I found I'd achieved maximum stability.

To put all of this into perspective, it's like trying to pee into a coffee can while riding a roller coaster at an amusement park.

The Magic Box

While in Japan, a woman traveling with me came out of the ladies room laughing. Normally bathroom experiences aren't supposed to be funny, but…

She began to describe the electrical boxes on the wall of each stall. The purpose of these boxes is to conserve water in the ladies room. The way it works is simple, you push a button and amplified toilet flushing sounds are produced for 15 seconds. After 10 seconds you get a warning light that the sounds will end shortly. This box is supposed to drown out any embarrassing sounds a woman might make while in the stall, without actually using any water.

Wipe Out

While I was in Kuala Lumpur, I went out for lunch and then decided I'd do some souvenir shopping before my flight later that evening. I'd been out for about an hour and had picked up two music boxes for a girlfriend. I also needed to find some scarves for one of my neighbors. She'd asked me to find a special type of scarf for her collection.

After finally finding and purchasing the scarf, my body informed me that I needed to make a trip to the restroom pretty darned quick. Normally when I travel, the last thing that I want to do is use a public toilet instead of the one at the hotel. Unfortunately I was not afforded that luxury on this occasion.

So I headed off to find a public restroom. Finally after about 10 minutes and near panic, I found one. Not to get into specific details, but I think this was the worst smelling and dirtiest restroom I'd ever visited — and this includes some frat house restrooms I've used.

While in the stall thinking there couldn't be any worse place to be, I soon discovered there was a new and unexpected obstacle I had to overcome. One piece of information that would have been extremely valuable to know was that public restrooms in Kuala Lumpur don't provide toilet paper of any kind. At this point, I was thinking this could leave a "real mess" on my hands.

Trying to maintain my dignity, I realized yelling for help was not on my list of options. After a couple minutes of thinking, I finally reached a decision…and my neighbor loved her music box.

The Toilet Tango

As we go through life, we face many tough questions that are sometimes difficult to answer. Things like, Is there a God? What's outside our universe? Will the Cubs ever win a World Series? These are questions many men have gone to their graves unable to answer.

I have one question that affects thousands of travelers every day, and still no one has been able to solve the mystery: "Why do the doors on bathroom stalls at airports open inward?"

If you travel at all, you've probably encountered this conundrum. If you need to use a stall, you'll invariably spend a few minutes doing the "Toilet Tango" with your carry-on luggage in order to get into the stall, set down your luggage, and then close the door.

Some travelers may not have the extra time to formulate a game plan just so they can use the toilet. Not to mention, if the toilet has an "auto sensor," it will get confused by all of the extra movement and just start randomly flushing. If the doors opened outward, entry and exit would be so much easier.

Road Hazards

When I travel, there are times when it seems almost impossible to find a toilet when I really need one. Then again, there was one time when the toilet actually found me.

I was on my third day of teaching a class in California when I decided to take a break from the normal routine of room service and go out for my meal. My lunchtime destination was just up the freeway from where I was staying.

When you drive on just about any major highway in California, most of the time you're surrounded by many large trucks. That day was no exception. I was on Interstate 580 in Livermore and had just changed lanes to begin my exit.

I got behind a flatbed truck as I drove along waiting for my exit to appear. *The load of Porta Pottys in the back of that truck in front of me doesn't look very stable,* I mused. I'd barely completed the thought, when one of the Porta Pottys fell off the side of the truck and went bouncing into the grass along the road. I watched it roll out of view and laughed.

I looked back at the road just as a second one fell off the back of the truck. Unfortunately, this one was positioned to hit my rent-a-car dead center. I don't know if you've ever had an outhouse approach you at 70 mph, if you have you know you're not allowed much time to make a decision, react, and control your bodily functions before disaster strikes.

I didn't have the time to develop an evasive strategy and execute it. I had a split second to make a "gut" decision and for some reason, I just swerved to my left, which was good because the outhouse bounced to my right.

Once I reached my exit, I pulled over to let my heart rate return to normal and to make sure I hadn't "soiled" my pants. After I regained my composure, I began thinking about how my expense report would've read if I'd gone to my right.

Foreign Objects

Sometimes you see the same thing time after time and think nothing of it. Then, one day you see it from an entirely different perspective and it changes everything. This happened to me in the men's room at the Los Angeles International Airport.

Each time I went in the restroom, I saw the same sign that read "Please do not throw *foreign objects* into the urinal." Suddenly, this took on a whole new meaning. Does this sign lead a visitor from another country to believe that we're really picky about what gets thrown into our toilets, and that we only want U.S. made objects in our urinals?

COMMUNICATION

*…She looked at me like I'd just said,
"There's a squirrel and a tomato playing poker on my tractor."*

Communication can be another major obstacle when traveling. You practice hard to learn a special phrase in Chinese to impress your hosts. Then, when the time comes for you to make a toast, you try to say, "To very good friends," and the room goes silent. This is because you've actually said, "You are all very fat."

Hotel management is good at selective communication. They have no problem informing you that you need to pay your bill at the halfway point of your stay. It's a totally different story when you try to tell them there are spiders in your room. They'll pretend they don't understand what you're saying. This is because they know some form of entertainment is coming their way.

In an effort to make them understand, you begin making spider puppets with your hands while making little spider noises (as if I know what spiders sound like), or you draw something that looks like a deformed squid and point to it. They nod to let you think they understand your silly gestures, and then they point you to the restaurant.

Contrary to popular belief, if the person you are talking to doesn't understand the first time, it *doesn't* help if you talk louder and slower.

I Need Deodorant

When your trip ends up lasting longer than you expected, you eventually have to purchase the personal items you can't live without, like toothpaste, deodorant, mouthwash, and chocolate covered almonds.

On a trip to Japan, I found myself in need of deodorant. I went into a nearby grocery store and searched for 10 minutes before coming to the conclusion that I'd have to ask for assistance. When the store clerks see you're foreign and about to ask a question, they scatter to all corners of the building (very similar to what happens when you turn on a light in a roach-infested room).

I finally cornered an older lady who couldn't move very fast and began my communication attempt. The first thing I say is, "Deodorant?" She looked at me like I'd just said, "There's a squirrel and a tomato playing poker on my tractor." She didn't have a clue.

So, now it's time for phase two. Relieved that no spiders are involved, I made the motion like I was putting on deodorant. She said something back to me and repeated my gesture. I nodded my head and thought, *That was easy.*

She began leading me around the store going by all of her coworkers pointing at me and making my deodorant gesture. Finally, when we got to the end of our journey, I came to an embarrassing realization. She thought I wanted to shave my armpits and brought me to the razors. I just hope that one day I don't have to ask for hemorrhoid cream.

No translation problem in Germany

Back Rub

After a rather long day at work, I went back to my hotel to take a brief nap before going to the hotel's happy hour. After all, I don't want to be tired when they're serving free beer and food.

Shortly into my slumber, I was awakened by a knock at the door. I got out of bed and walked toward the door. I responded to the knock by saying, "Yes?"

I heard a man's voice saying, "Back rub."

Not quite the response I was expecting and perhaps I was still partially asleep, so I asked again. I got the same response. I yelled through the door, "I didn't order a back rub. Please, go away."

There was about a 10 second pause and then there was another knock at the door. "Housekeeping, do you want back rub?"

At this point, I feel like I'm living a skit from *Saturday Night Live*. I looked through the peephole on the door and saw a man wearing a hotel uniform, so I simply said, "No, thank you."

The man yells back, "I must deliver back rub."

I am upset now, and opened the door to tell him what I thought of him and his back rub. Once the door was open, there was a Hispanic man holding a bathrobe standing in front of me. He was trying to give me a *bathrobe* not a back rub. I apologized for being rude and he smiled.

I closed the door and as I was getting ready to resume my nap, I hear from the room next door: Knock-Knock-Knock… "Back rub."

You Go First

As soon as I learn a new phrase in a foreign language, I'm always pretty eager to try it out. In Japan, I was taught the phrase to say when you want someone to "go ahead" or "go first." I learned the phrase from my host while we were having dinner.

I practiced it all night long, eagerly awaiting the first opportunity to use it. Finally, the opportunity presented itself. I was in the hotel elevator with a Japanese gentleman. When we reached the ground floor, the doors opened and I held my hand toward the door, then said my newly learned phrase asking him to "go ahead" and leave the elevator first.

I stood there with a feeling of accomplishment and was quite proud of the fact that I'd communicated in Japanese. The man just looked at me strangely, smiled and exited the elevator. I knew I'd said it correctly, but something wasn't right.

Later that day, I asked my host what I'd done wrong. When I described the situation to him, he started laughing. It turns out the phrase I was using should only be used when food arrives and you want the other person to "go ahead" and start eating. No wonder the gentleman in the elevator looked confused.

"State" of Mind

Believe it or not, there are times when I'm not the focal point of an embarrassing situation. It's definitely comforting for me to witness the "bizarre" happening to someone else. Watching others experience a "travel meltdown" assures me that I'm not alone when it comes to having my special moments. It's even better when it happens to someone in their own country speaking their native language.

These situations are usually few and far between, but when they do happen, I enjoy the moment and feel better knowing that I'm not the only person who occasionally forgets to "pack his brain" when he travels.

Around 8 a.m. one Sunday morning, I was preparing to go to a football game. Getting together with friends to BBQ and drink beer has been a longtime pre-game tailgating ritual.

Before I left for the game, I went to the local grocery store because there were a few supplies I still needed to buy. I'd already bought my beer the night before because at that time in Arizona you weren't allowed to buy alcohol on Sunday mornings before 10 a.m.

I gathered my stuff and headed for the checkout stand. As I stood in line waiting to pay for my items, I noticed the gentleman in front of me had a 12-pack of beer. I got his attention and politely said, "Excuse me, are you aware you can't buy alcohol in Arizona before 10 o'clock?"

He looked at me for a second, thought about what I'd just said, then replied, "It's okay, I'm from California."

Of all of the possible responses I'd expected to hear, that one was not on my list. I was caught so off guard by his statement that I couldn't even think of a comeback. All I knew was the next few minutes should be pretty interesting.

Once the man was at the front of the line, he set the beer down in front of the cashier and waited to be charged for his 12-pack. As soon as the cashier saw the beer, she looked at him and said, "I hate to ruin the party, but you can't buy your beer until 10 o'clock."

The man pulled out his wallet and showed her his driver's license. She looked at it and said, "What would you like me to do with that?"

He confidently looked at her and said, "I'm from California, and we can buy beer at any time on Sundays."

After hearing this, the cashier (a friend of mine) briefly looked through him and at me. I just stood there with a smile, knowing that what was coming was going to be worth the "price of admission."

After the man told the cashier he was from California, the following discussion took place:

Cashier: "What state do you think we're in?"
Man: "Arizona."
Cashier: "Right. In Arizona you can't buy beer before 10 a.m."
Man: "Those rules apply to people from Arizona. I'm from California."
Cashier: "I'm sorry, but I can't sell you this beer."
Man: "You're wrong! I want to talk to your manager."

A couple of minutes passed and the store manager joined the conversation. The man trying to buy the beer said to the manager, "Will you tell your cashier that people in California can buy beer at any time on Sundays."

The manager acknowledged his statement with a nod of his head, looked at the cashier and said, "He is correct, people in California can buy beer at any time on Sundays." The manager briefly paused and then continued, "However, he is in Arizona not California; don't sell him the beer."

With that, the manager walked away. The man realized he wasn't going to be purchasing any beer for the moment, looked at the cashier and said, "People in Arizona are stupid."

Customer Service, Defined

During a one-month stay in Osaka Japan, I found a little restaurant that became kind of special to me. It was a family-run business, and I ate there an average of four nights a week. The thing that made this place special was the only English that they understood was, "Check please" and "Thank you."

After a few visits, one of the owners, a chubby lady in her late 50s or early 60s, decided that I was her "special project." Every time I walked into the building, she'd pull my business card out of her wallet, hold it next to her heart and then point at me indicating she wanted me to sit in her section.

Once seated, she'd bring me a large bottle of beer, an incredibly small glass, and an appetizer — all without me having to say a word.

There's a custom in Japan that says when you're among friends you're not allowed to pour your own beer. At most restaurants, you're given a small glass for your beer. The purpose of the small glass is so you can make many toasts with the people you're with. I rarely had anyone with me to share a toast; therefore, my glass was always in need of a refill.

Whenever it looked like I was ready to refill my glass, the owner would almost fly across the room to make sure I didn't have to pour my own beer. There were a couple of times when she actually knocked over chairs in order to get to my glass before I made the attempt.

The menus at this restaurant were all written in Japanese with no English assistance. This made it difficult to know what I was ordering.

One day, she handed me a photocopy of their menu and a pencil. She took me around to tables where people were eating various dishes and pointed them out on the menu. I'd then write down my description of the meal so I'd know what it was when I ordered next time.

The only problem with this system was even though she was pointing to different lines on the menu, all of the dishes looked the same to me — fish, rice, and noodles!

In this type of restaurant, once you place your order it's delivered to the kitchen by your waitress, who is yelling at the top of her lungs for the cooks to hear. This can sound really confusing when three or four waitresses are all yelling out orders at the same time. *How are they going to get this right?* I wondered. Then, I remembered all the dishes look alike, so I guess it didn't really matter.

Every night after I finished my dinner, the waitress would send her son to the corner drug store for a small carton of ice cream for me. When things got slow, she'd sit down with me for what I thought was the best part of the whole evening. We began to talk to each other by drawing pictures, using facial or hand gestures, and grunting. I felt like a caveman only with nicer clothes.

We covered a variety of topics. Early on, I explained that I'd been to the zoo. I drew pictures of a monkey, zebra, and a lion. She looked at me and then shook her head no. I was the one at the zoo, I knew what I saw, so I responded by nodding my head yes. I found out later that she thought I was drawing my pets back home.

One night she managed to ask me if I wanted to go and pick grapes with her family the next morning. It sounded interesting, but picking grapes at 5:30 on a Sunday morning didn't sound like my idea of fun, so I respectfully declined.

It's All a Matter of Interpretation

In the United States, most of us have the ability to communicate amongst ourselves and typically be successful at getting our messages across. If you sit down in a restaurant and order a steak, chances are good that your waiter won't walk away thinking you want a plate full of butter. More than likely you'll get exactly what you asked for — therefore your communication was successful.

Knowing early on in school that I was much too dangerous with tools to be in any shop class, I decided to take Spanish as my elective. I figured Spanish would be beneficial to me once I got older and joined the workforce (at least that's what I'd been told). Today, I spend 80% of my time in Asia and for some strange reason I'm finding my knowledge of Spanish less than helpful when I'm teaching a room full of Chinese students.

Many times I have to work with interpreters to succeed at communicating. I usually have a small core group of people that assist me during my classes. I've learned over the years that there are good interpreters, bad interpreters, and some people who should be limited to cleaning the lint traps at the local Laundromat.

Occasionally the people I'm used to working with aren't available and a replacement is offered (a.k.a. the sacrificial lamb). Switching interpreters midstream is like replacing your dance partner of three years with your landscaper. It inevitably creates awkward moments.

During my first day of training for a Korean customer, I was working with a new interpreter. We got through the introductions without any problems, and I was ready to start the teaching portion of my class. I simply said, "Okay, let's get going."

The next thing I know, my students are walking out the door. My interpreter thought I was dismissing the class for a break, so he told them to leave.

In Japan, I was teaching my class how to use the machine my company sells. I'd just finished explaining a particular calibration step and gave the okay for my interpreter to repeat what I'd said. He spoke for a while and the students asked him questions. This exchange continued for about five minutes.

I'm feeling pretty good about what I'm seeing and hearing. However, that didn't last long. A moment later they stop talking, the students look at me, and my interpreter turns to me and asks, "How big is your house in Phoenix?"

I asked him what that had to do with calibrating a piece of equipment. His reply was that he didn't fully understand what I'd said so they had a group discussion about my house.

When you have to work with an interpreter, it's important to go over the script and practice instead of working from a "cold start." A little time spent up front will prevent awkward moments like these, and prevent having to teach your interpreter on your audience's time.

I've lost count of how many times I've asked my students questions via my interpreter, only to have him answer the question because he thought I was asking him directly. Practice time will allow you to develop your routine as a team.

After you complete a session, you don't want to be remembered as the two guys who performed the Asian version of "Who's on First?" Remember that an interpreter is there to help you. The best thing you can do for them is to make it as easy as possible to translate your words.

If you're working with an interpreter who's not used to your style, the use of slang and unfamiliar words is something to be avoided whenever possible. Many interpreters hear slang and create a sentence based on the one or two words they recognize, usually resulting in something like: Warning: Remove the monkey from the bicycle before talking to the birthday cake.

Top This

On one trip, I spent 10 days in Ireland and never saw the sun. When the Ireland business was completed, my next stop was in the eastern part of Germany, where I did get to see the sun but the average outside temperature was minus 17 degrees during the day. It was too cold to venture outside at night, so all of my meals during my week-long stay were eaten at the hotel restaurant or bar.

On my final night in Germany, I was sitting at the bar when the gentleman next to me ordered a pizza. I looked over when his meal arrived and thought the pizza looked pretty darned good. I figured ordering it wouldn't be a problem because there was a picture of it on the menu.

However, I couldn't leave well enough alone. I had to turn it into the non-standard product by trying to order extra toppings. The only English the lady behind the bar knew was, "You're welcome," when she delivered my beer, and she always said it before I could say, "Thank you."

When I asked for additional toppings on my pizza, she didn't understand what I wanted. She got her assistant and asked me to repeat my request. I said, "Extra toppings, please." The assistant didn't understand either, so he brought the bar manager into the conversation.

By this time, I'm trying to tell them never mind, but they insisted on helping me. So, for a third time I asked for extra toppings. Since the entire bar staff was trying to figure out what I wanted, I grabbed the menu and started pointing at the toppings, asking for more cheese, more meat, more mushrooms, etc.

All of a sudden the "light bulb" comes on and the three of them say in unison, "Ah, toppers." Finally, communication had been achieved. After a few head nods and smiles, the bartender was able to place my pizza order and ask for my extra toppers.

I sat there for about 15 minutes, until the bartender and her assistant came back from the kitchen. The bartender put the rather plain pizza in front of me. Then, her assistant handed me five bowls of different toppers. I guess it was wrong for me to assume that they knew I wanted my "toppers" on the pizza.

Beer with a Friend

After a one-hour train ride and then a walk back to my hotel in Osaka, I decided to take a quick nap before meeting my coworker, Lee, for dinner. About 45 minutes into my nap, I was awakened by the sound of sirens just outside my window. I continued lying there, figuring they'd eventually go on by the hotel.

After about 10 minutes of sirens, I smelled smoke. I got up and pulled back the curtains only to see three fire trucks and several police cars in front of the hotel. Flames were coming out of the building across the street in front of the hotel. They were shooting about 20–30 feet into the air.

Once the excitement died down, I called Lee's room and we decided to escape the smell of smoke and go for dinner at a nearby restaurant. The dinner was uneventful until we were just about ready to pay the bill and leave.

While we were sitting there, a man (who was obviously very drunk) came up to us with a beer in his hand and pointed at our table while speaking to us in Japanese. Neither Lee nor I knew what he wanted.

We shook our heads in an attempt to tell him we didn't understand what he was trying to tell us. He still kept speaking Japanese and pointing to our table. I spoke to him in Japanese, saying we didn't understand, but he kept on pointing at our table.

Just another "Round-Up" in Japan

I picked up an ashtray and tried to hand it to him; he didn't want the ashtray. I picked up some chopsticks and tried to give those to him; once again, that apparently was not what he wanted. Just then, a waitress walked by and Lee got her to figure out what the man wanted. It turned out he wanted to buy us a beer.

We accepted his offer, but little did we realize that this meant that he was now going to sit with us and continue to speak Japanese. He just kept speaking, and I kept repeating "wakarimasen" which is Japanese for I don't understand.

We learned the man had the same belief many Americans hold: if someone doesn't understand, speak louder and slower. He'd bring his face very close to ours and speak. Half the time, it seemed like he was about to fall asleep in mid-sentence, and the alcohol on his breath was overpowering. We kept shaking our heads and telling him we didn't understand.

The man made gestures like he wanted us to go with him. It appeared he wanted us to either go to another bar or to dance with him. Once again, our reply was that we didn't understand.

Finally, after about 10 minutes of this, we gave up and started responding to him in English. We had no idea what he was saying but we played along and answered his questions. We were quite sure he was just as clueless about what we were saying as we were about his comments. He just kept getting louder, and many of the restaurant's patrons enjoyed watching our little sideshow.

This seemingly endless dialog continued for a few minutes. Then, we finished our beers and said good-bye to our new friend.

When Lee and I returned to the restaurant a few days later, two of the waitresses came over and told us they remembered our "sideshow" and thought we were brave. I'm sure our buddy doesn't remember us, but we'll never forget him.

PHOTO COURTESY OF SPENCER CHUNG

TRANSPORTATION

"...Singapore has one million cars and only four open parking spaces available at any one given time."

Elevators

Elevators present a different challenge when you're outside the U.S. The first thing you'll notice in Asia is there is always someone who feels it's their God-given right to be in charge of the elevator doors.

As soon as the doors open, they stand directly in front of the control panel and guard those precious open and close buttons. When the elevator stops, they'll hit the "close door" button immediately, meaning you have about three seconds to force your way out of the elevator or you'll end up visiting all of the other floors in that particular building. This process continues until a mass exit eventually sucks the "button-pusher" out on one of the floors.

In the US, four or five people get on an elevator and it seems crowded. The goal in Asia seems to be to cram an entire village plus livestock (smell permitting) into one elevator. The elevator loading procedure is simple. Everybody packs into the elevator until the "overweight alarm" sounds. Then, people get off one at a time until the alarm stops.

Tragically, some families occasionally get separated for weeks because of this procedure and the person in control of the buttons.

Elevators in Korea

Just about every item on the Korean menu involves heavy doses of garlic. I love garlic and I'd probably wear garlic deodorant if they made it. However, garlic on the breath of someone else is a totally different story.

When 20 people and a chicken join you in an elevator after eating lunch, you'll do everything in your power not to inhale. If you're headed for the 40th floor, you may have to exit two or three times, just to breathe, before you reach your final destination. I think the purpose of the chicken is to act as some sort of air freshener.

All elevator rules for loading and unloading apply on the subways in Asia as well. The only difference is you move sideways instead of up and down.

Elevator Etiquette

On one trip, I was at a hotel in Germany waiting for an elevator to take me downstairs. When the doors opened, I saw that two Japanese gentlemen were already onboard. The elevator stopping for me on the eighth floor must've caught them off guard because they both got off as I got on.

Before the doors closed, they realized they weren't in the lobby; so one guy jumped back and held the doors to keep them from closing. The two men then got back on the elevator. For some reason for the entire ride down to the lobby, they seemed to feel they had to "reprogram" the elevator at each floor.

In Germany, the letter "E" on the elevator panel means lobby. It seemed like a simple concept to me, which is why I don't have a clue why these guys started hitting all of the floor buttons between the eighth floor and the lobby. Every time the doors opened, they got out only to realize they weren't in the lobby, then they'd jump back on. It was almost like they were riding the elevator for the first time.

When we got to the second floor, four of their colleagues were standing there as the doors opened. The men on the outside were definitely senior to the two guys in the elevator with me. I soon learned that even though we were in Germany, all Japanese rules of etiquette still applied. The guys in the elevator bowed, then the guys outside the elevator bowed. Then, they exchanged bows again and again. I think at one point I even felt the need to bow.

The next etiquette rule to be enforced was allowing the senior guys to ride to the lobby ahead of the guys who were already in the elevator. Before I knew it, some sort passenger exchange "cha-cha" was taking place in this extremely small elevator — the guys who were in got out and the guys who were out got in. Then, the whole bowing process started all over again.

I decided to break up the bowing party by saying, "Excuse me," and pressing the button to close the elevator doors. After the doors closed, the senior guys looked at me like I'd done something extremely rude. I guess they just didn't realize I couldn't participate in their lengthy rituals — I had an airplane to catch in 36 hours.

Getting Around

The most common form of transportation while traveling on business is the taxi. Common as they are, they also provide entertainment, excitement, and a whole lot of fear.

In Indonesia, a taxi is a used vehicle the rest of the world *doesn't want*. Some countries sink unwanted cars in the ocean. Indonesians fish them out of the water and turn them into taxis.

On one trip, my driver greeted me and I got into his cab. Immediately the driver grabbed a rope and tied my door shut. When I looked down, I noticed I could see the ground between my feet. *This must be Fred Flintstone's old car,* I thought with a little trepidation.

In Korea you'll see many tour busses as they wait in traffic with you. All of a sudden you'll notice that some of the busses are bouncing up and down while the vehicle is at a total standstill. I found out these are Karaoke busses, complete with dance floor and bar.

In the Philippines, you have a choice of taking a Taxi or a Jeepney. A Jeepney is like a Jeep station wagon covered in lights, speakers, reflectors, signs, and Jesus statues. You jump in the back and get out when you think you're near your destination. If you ask how many people can fit into a Jeepney, the reply is always, "One more!"

It's common to be stuck in traffic in the Philippines waiting for water buffalo to get off the road. I've also noticed that taxi drivers in the Philippines all have a second profession. These range from bartending to running a dating service. They practice their second job while driving and quite often lose track of the primary objective, DRIVING SAFELY!

My vote for one of the most interesting places to drive would go to Taiwan. The combination of mopeds, pedestrians, and cars must be witnessed to be believed. Traffic lights, road lines, and "One Way" signs are only taken as suggestions.

To make a left hand turn in Taiwan, you move to the front of all of the stopped cars and aim towards the direction you wish to turn. When the time is right, all cars pointed in that direction take off at the same

Time Zones, Beer & Left-Handed Chopsticks

Typical traffic light in Taiwan

time, which usually ends up being five cars trying to merge into one lane. Right of way is based entirely on gross weight. People yield to mopeds, mopeds yield to cars, and cars yield to oversized military vehicles. Every traffic light is like the start of a motorcycle race. I think the law in Taiwan states that it's okay to drive on the sidewalk under the following two conditions:

1. You are operating a motorized vehicle.
2. You are in Taiwan

Parking in Singapore

Singapore is beautiful and one of my favorite places to visit. My recommendation for getting around here is to take a taxi, bus, or the subway. *Do not rent a car!*

Singapore has one million cars and only four open parking spaces are available at any given time. If you want to drive somewhere to have dinner, you must leave shortly after lunch so you can find a parking place by dinnertime.

Singapore is the only place I know of where you can actually burn a half tank of gas just looking for a parking space. Once you've found one, you must make sure you have the right type of parking permit displayed on your dash or your car won't be there when you return.

Where Are We Going?

I was in my seventh week of an eight-week stay in the Philippines when I noticed my taxi driver was taking a path back to my hotel that was unfamiliar to me. After 7 weeks, I knew just about every possible route a taxi driver could take to get from where I was teaching to my hotel.

No matter which route my taxi driver took, there were two distinct landmarks we always passed, which always assured me we were headed in the right direction. The first landmark was a big pile of burning garbage next to a school. The smell of which was enough to turn your stomach inside out. The second landmark was a sign that read "Tire Vulcanizing and Dentist Here."

After realizing we weren't going anywhere near my intended destination, the following conversation took place:

Me: "Where are we going?"
Taxi Driver: "Oh, we go get you a woman."
Me: "What?"
Taxi Driver: "I said, we go get you a woman."
Me: "I don't want a woman."
Taxi Driver: "You don't want woman?"
Me: "Correct, I do not want a woman!"
Taxi Driver: "You want man?"

Me:	"No! I do not want a man, a woman, a child, or an animal. I just want to get back to the hotel and have a beer."
Taxi Driver:	"You want beer?"
Me:	"Yes."
Taxi Driver:	"Okay, we go get you a beer and then we go get you a woman."

At that point, we were stopped at a light. I threw 40 pesos over the seat and jumped out of the cab. This was the only time I'd experienced this sort of adventure. I was beginning to get nervous and my instincts told me to get out now. When you're unsure of the situation, I've learned it's always best to follow your instincts.

Most cab rides in the Philippines involve a one-sided conversation where the driver just starts telling you stories about their country and how proud they are of it — they don't try to find women for you!

Two of a Kind?

After arriving in Taiwan, I walked out of customs around 10 p.m. and went directly to the area where the limo drivers wait for their scheduled rides. As I approached the area, I saw a man holding a sign that read, "Mr. Bruce." I walked over to him and presented him with a business card for the limo company that was scheduled for me.

He acknowledged that he worked for the company by pointing to himself. I mentioned the city name of my intended destination, which was 45 minutes away from the airport. He smiled and held up the Mr. Bruce sign again.

Even though drivers are told where to go when reservations are made, it never hurts to confirm the final destination before leaving the airport. We loaded my stuff into his car and away we went.

As we drove along, I began to notice the scenery looked different than what I was used to seeing on my previous trips. I thought perhaps we were taking some back roads to avoid the freeway traffic. After about 25 minutes, I came to the conclusion that we were not going anywhere near where I wanted to be.

So, once again, I said the name of the city (Hsin-Chu). This time, he pulls the car off to the side of the road and holds up the Mr. Bruce sign, wanting to make sure that I was Bruce.

He didn't speak English and I don't speak Chinese, but the two of us quickly figured out something wasn't right. He promptly got on the phone to his boss, while I phoned the person who made my reservation.

When all of the confusion had settled, it turned out that this privately owned limo company had two pick-ups named Bruce at the same time in the same location. One of us had a 45-minute ride and the other had a 30-minute ride in a different direction.

Unfortunately for me, I found the wrong driver. The one I should've found spoke English. That driver and his Bruce figured out their mismatch and never left the airport.

Now, here is where things got strange. I was 25 minutes into a 45-minute ride and the dispatcher for the limo company decided that it would be better to have both drivers meet back at the airport to have the Bruce exchange. This meant Bruce #2 had to wait another 25 minutes for me to return to the airport so that he and his assigned, driver could complete their route as planned.

For me, this meant instead of just getting on the freeway and finishing the journey, I had to go back to the airport and restart my whole trip. When I got back to the airport, I met the other Mr. Bruce, got the right driver and finally made it to my apartment in Hsin-Chu around 12:30 a.m.

Nice Day, Huh?

I was in Korea just a few days before the 1988 Olympics. During this period, Korea was going through all sorts of practices so a visitor to their country would feel comfortable. One of the practices was to take dog meat off the menus at restaurants featuring western style cooking, like Denny's.

Another practice was to have the cab drivers learn foreign languages. One day, I got into a cab and the driver greeted me by asking if I was American. When I responded yes, he fumbled around in a box of cassette tapes until he found the one he wanted. He inserted the tape into the player and just like that, I'm listening to the soundtrack to *Saturday Night Fever*.

We drove for a couple of minutes, then he looked back at me through the rear view mirror and said, "John Travolta is a really good dancer." Then he emphasized his statement by giving me the "thumbs up" gesture.

Later on, during the same ride, he turned down the volume on the radio and said, "Excuse me." I look up and he said, "It's a very nice day today, sir. Don't you think so?"

I had a big smile on my face and he was afraid that he'd said something incorrectly. I assured him he'd said it beautifully and then gave him the "thumbs up" gesture. I then told him that the way we'd say it in the U.S. would be simply, "Nice day, huh?"

He tried it once, I coached him a little, and then he looked at me and said, "Much easier!"

The next morning, I got into a cab at the hotel. The cab was from the same company, but with a different driver. I was immediately greeted with, "Nice day, huh?" Then, when I left work that afternoon, I was greeted once again by another driver with that now all too familiar phrase, "Nice day, huh?"

I guess they must've had some sort of network where they shared information on how to speak to foreigners. I'd like to catch up with the person who told them the soundtrack to *Saturday Night Fever* was an American favorite!

One Way Street?

I think all taxi drivers in the Philippines believe you're indestructible if you have a Jesus statue on your dashboard. There's also an unwritten code among these drivers giving them permission to change driving rules to meet their immediate needs.

I'd been warned about the taxi route back to the hotel when leaving one particular customer in downtown Manila. I'd been on some pretty scary taxi rides before and thought there was nothing a taxi driver in the Philippines could do to make me nervous. Boy, was I wrong!

When leaving this particular customer's site, the proper route is to make a right hand turn onto a one way street, drive for about a half mile, make two left turns and then head back toward the hotel. This process usually takes about 10 minutes, depending on traffic conditions.

In the Philippine taxi driver-amended version, the process only takes a couple of minutes. They start out by going left on the one-way street, directly into oncoming traffic for a distance of about 200 yards.

On a good day, they'll stay on the shoulder of the road; otherwise, you'll end up squeezing between some busses. Then, they make a left turn onto another one-way street into more oncoming traffic, followed by an immediate U-turn. The U-turn is followed by a left turn in the proper direction, going with the traffic flow.

The first time this happened, I began to pray in languages I don't even speak. After six weeks of doing this every day, the excitement level for me was reduced to that of a third grade music recital.

The most entertaining part of these rides was when I accompanied my coworkers on their first ride back to the hotel. I didn't warn them about what to expect; I just watched their faces as they saw their lives pass before their eyes.

Just Say No

Osaka, Japan has a specialized taxi company that strives to give you a limousine feel and service whenever you ride with them. One of the amenities is a packet of tissue, ceremoniously handed over by your driver. The first time this happened, I thought it was nice. But, when you're in Japan for three weeks and you take a taxi three or four times a day, receiving a packet each time —it gets to be a bit much.

These packets peacefully sit dormant throughout the remainder of your trip. Then, once you've made it home, they appear out of nowhere and haunt you until the end of time. I've even found them in the pockets of a jacket I didn't remember wearing. I almost expect to find one in my mailbox or even my refrigerator! I'm almost afraid to throw them away, because the remaining tissues might sense it and start to multiply.

My advice to you is when your taxi driver turns around to hand you that first packet of tissues, you can do one of two things — run screaming from the taxi and take a city bus instead, or maybe just politely say, "No, thank you," and avoid the whole mess.

May I Take Your Bag?

American Tourister used to have a commercial that showed the durability of their luggage by putting it in a cage with a couple of gorillas. Since I've been traveling, I've learned they took the easy way out. If they really wanted to torture their suitcases, they should've brought them to Asia and let a few Taiwanese taxi drivers take them for a spin.

I'd had to replace my oversized suitcase because it developed a irreparable case of SCS, otherwise known as Shopping Cart Syndrome — the condition where one wheel freezes and makes steering nearly impossible, sending you crashing into 400 jars of neatly stacked mustard bottles sitting in the center of the aisle. When a wheel on your suitcase does this in a foreign airport, the police automatically think you're on drugs and start following you.

Anyway, I arrived in Taipei, exited customs, and found the driver assigned to take me to the hotel. My driver was an old man. I'm not sure how old he was, but I'm willing to bet he was present at the first sunrise on earth.

I had two pieces of luggage with me. One was my brand new oversized suitcase and the other was my computer briefcase. I tried to hand him the smaller bag, but he insisted on taking the large one, which weighed as much as he did.

As we walked toward the parking lot, the first thing we encountered was a set of stairs. Halfway up the stairs, the bag slipped out of his hand and crashed down about seven or eight steps. He refused to let me get the bag for him, and proceeded to drag it back up the stairs on its side.

I helplessly watched my brand new suitcase bang, bounce and roll on the stairs as he dragged it along. Once we finally made it to the parking lot, he tried to ask me how my flight was as we walked. Apparently, he was trying to concentrate on my answer and not really paying attention to where he was walking.

All of a sudden, he caught my suitcase on the front license plate of a parked car. The license plate was torn from the car, the bag came out of his hands, and once again my new suitcase was back on the ground. In seconds we were up and rolling again, which led me to believe he'd done this many times.

Once we got to his car, he insisted on putting my bag the trunk without any assistance. He opened his trunk and I noticed it was already full of luggage. He stood there for a moment looking puzzled, he muttered something in Chinese, and then he told me he'd forgotten to give his last passenger his luggage.

Since the trunk was full, he crammed my bags into the back seat. I got into the cab, and we headed for the hotel. When we arrived, I made sure I grabbed both of my bags, and went inside. I checked in, and then went up to my room.

I'd been in my room for about 10 minutes when there was a knock at the door. When I opened the door, there was the Bell Captain and all of the luggage I'd seen in the trunk of my taxi. He told me the taxi driver came back and said he'd forgotten to give me my luggage.

I told the Bell Captain it wasn't my luggage. He looked at me like I was crazy. He asked if I was sure it wasn't mine. At this point, I

PHOTO COURTESY OF ROD SCHWARTZ

In China, a water taxi is usually available if you're not in a hurry.

began to wonder how I was going to convince him and get him to take the bags back downstairs with him. Finally, after a few awkward moments, I convinced him and he left.

The next morning while I was checking out, I saw the homeless bags sitting behind the counter. I couldn't help but think those bags would probably never see their rightful owner again, since the only connection to finding their owner was a short Asian man with dark hair and glasses who drives a yellow taxi...

Come Blow Your Horn

When purchasing a car in Asia, taking it for a test drive isn't as important to most people as testing the functionality of the horn.

Being stuck in a traffic jam or in severe gridlock usually occupies most of your time while driving an Asian automobile, so the horn is a pretty important means of communication.

I've been a witness to some creative maneuvers that many stuntmen would be afraid to try. For example, a driver attempting a five lane U-turn while eating a bowl of noodles and talking on his cell phone is very common. Or, someone may feel it's necessary to drive against traffic in order to save time. These attempts usually end in some sort of failure where the end solution requires a police officer and a tow truck.

The traffic jams are also epic. Even when it's obvious to the world that you won't be moving for the next few minutes, the driver behind you usually thinks differently and feels he needs to make you aware of the fact by blasting his horn in three-second long bleats, repeatedly. He will continue to do this until either his battery dies or he becomes an unwilling participant in some sort of mob violence.

If there's the slightest bit of space available in front of your vehicle, the person behind you will try to move in front of you and take it. Before he can get there, though, the space is quickly filled by three (or nine) motor scooters. The addition of the scooters provides the same function to traffic as cement to building a brick wall. So, now, the only thing left for you to do is blow your horn at everyone else in the vicinity.

Just to further the importance of the horn, I recall a time when I was in the Philippines and my taxi driver's horn stopped functioning. He pulled off to the side of the road, stuck his hand behind the steering column and pulled out a wire. He touched the wire to the dashboard and the horn functioned perfectly. He continued to steer with his left hand and operate the horn wire with is right.

TAKE LUGGAGE OF FOREIGNER

NO CHARGE

提行李處

LOST LUGGAGE

*"...Knowing that clean underwear was just an elevator ride away,
I was the happiest man on the face of the earth."*

Airport "Debriefing"

I don't need to look for strange things; they find me in the simplest of circumstances. For example, I'd just completed a cruise with my family and was waiting for my luggage in baggage claim at Miami International Airport. I stood near the carousel, and had collected five of our six pieces of luggage. Ten minutes had passed since I grabbed bag five and I was beginning to wonder if I'd ever get to see bag six.

While standing almost on top of the conveyer belt, I turned to motion to my girlfriend about the missing bag. All of a sudden I felt a rather sharp tug on my shorts. My first response wasn't to move in the direction of the tug. Instead, I moved in the opposite direction. When I did this, my shorts were quickly jerked to knee level.

A hook from another passenger's garment bag was sticking out beyond the carousel and had managed to get caught on the inside of my shorts. When a 40-pound bag competes with a pair of 12-ounce shorts, the bag wins.

Trying not to make matters worse, I ran alongside the carousel with my shorts around my knees trying to disconnect the garment bag. This was the not too happy ending to a wonderful vacation. While the incident was a little embarrassing for me, it made a great dinner conversation topic for roughly 60 people who were now privy to my preference between boxers, briefs, or commando.

Luggage Detectives

I've been traveling for many years through many airports, and until recently my bags and I usually arrive in the same city, on the same day, at the same time.

My strategy is simple. If I'm renting a car, I'll usually check my bag. If not, I have a carry-on. My logic is that once I've convinced the car rental clerk I don't want a convertible in Vermont in January, my bag should be waiting for me at baggage claim. This has always worked well for me until my last trip to Allentown, Pennsylvania.

After getting the keys for my rental car, I walked over to baggage claim and noticed there was only one bag remaining on the carousel. It was similar to my bag, much the same way a Big Mac almost looks like a seafood buffet. It took no time for me to realize that someone had taken my bag by mistake and was on their way to their destination with it.

So, I did the next logical thing. Realizing that they have no control over this matter, I blamed the airline for losing my bag.

After filing a claim, I checked into my hotel and waited for the "Lost Luggage Detectives" to tell me they'd solved the case.

At 2 a.m., I was awakened by a phone call. It was a gentleman from the airline who told me I'd left the airport with the wrong bag. After thinking to myself, *Did this man's father marry his sister?* I explained to him that someone had taken *my bag* with *my clothes*. I also told him I'd left the airport with nothing but the clothes I'd been wearing for the last 16 hours.

I'd come on this trip to accompany our salesman on some customer visits. Now, I had to ask the clerk at the front desk for a toothbrush, razor, and comb so I could make myself look somewhat presentable.

At 7 a.m., I met our salesman, Andy, in the lobby. He was wearing slacks, a dress shirt, tie, and a nice coat. I was still in the same clothes I'd put on 21 hours earlier — jeans, sneakers, and polo shirt. What was worse, my hair was combed in a way that resembled a Troll Doll. Before leaving the hotel, I asked the desk clerk to tell housekeeping I had not checked out, it only looked that way.

We made our visits, apologized for my appearance, and got back to the hotel around 6 p.m. The desk clerk informed me that my bag had been found earlier in the day and it had been put in my room.

Knowing that clean underwear was now just an elevator ride away, I was the happiest man on the face of the earth. I walked into my room and my bag was nowhere to be found. I returned to the front desk to tell them my bag was not in my room, and they thought I was joking.

I was beginning to think this was some sort of Pennsylvania conspiracy, and I became quite vocal about my "found lost bag that was now lost again." They thought the bellboy might've put it in room 221 because I was in 321. They checked but found nothing. They also couldn't find the bellboy to ask him, because he'd left work three hours earlier.

At 9 p.m. they were finally able to reach him. Apparently, because it looked like nobody had checked into my room, he just assumed the front desk meant for him to put the bag in the room next to mine.

I finally got my bag, changed into clean clothes, and was very content. Two hours later, I got a call from the airline's "Lost Luggage Detectives" informing me they had just recovered my luggage and were driving it over to me as we speak. I definitely heard banjo music playing the theme from *Deliverance*.

Lost and Found

I was waiting for a flight at an airport in Florida when I heard a loud commotion at the gate across from me. When I looked over, there was a Hispanic family in a fully developed state of hysteria. The group consisted of about ten people who all seemed to be extremely emotional — if they weren't yelling at the gate agent in Spanish, they were crying.

I had some time to kill before my flight so I decided to satisfy my curiosity and see what was going on. I wandered over to the gate and found out the family was waiting for a casket to arrive. My first thought was, *Why are they waiting at the gate?*

The ruckus was over the fact that the casket was lost and the airline didn't have a clue where it was. The amount of Spanish I could understand was limited, but I sure understood how upset they were. Even though I wouldn't want to experience what this family was going through, the following thoughts immediately came to mind:

1. The phrase, "This man would be late for his own funeral."
2. Somewhere at some remote airport, a casket is going around unclaimed on the baggage carousel.

Broken Locks

As everyone knows, increased airport security means all checked baggage is now screened. During a trip to Singapore, airport security decided they had to open my luggage without me being present. Apparently, that gave them permission to cut the TSA-approved lock from my suitcase, making the lock totally unusable.

After going through everything that I spent time packing with care, they crammed my belongings back into the suitcase. It was painfully obvious that Airport Screener training doesn't include how to repack a suitcase.

On top of my freshly mangled clothing, they thoughtfully placed my broken lock in a plastic bag with a note attached advising me to use the nylon tie wraps that can be purchased at my local hardware store to secure my luggage in the future, instead of using a lock.

Think about this advice for a minute. In order for me to protect my belongings, I have to seal my luggage with something that requires a sharp tool to remove, but the law forbids me to carry that tool while I travel — it needs to be packed inside my secured luggage.

Going Out on "A Limb"

In Terminal 3 at Phoenix Sky Harbor Airport, they have a large glass case that's full of unclaimed luggage. In it you'll see many suitcases, a few child car seats, laptop computers, and I'm sure that if you searched hard enough, you might even find Jimmy Hoffa.

I can understand how some of these items become lost or misplaced, especially after a long flight. There was, however, one item I saw that still confuses me to this day. In the middle of the case, on a shelf all by itself, was an artificial leg. *How could someone check his or her leg and then "walk off" without it?* Personally, I think I'd get as far as one step before realizing my other leg was missing.

HOTELS

"...Your room is only confirmed based on availability at the time of your arrival."

While staying at a nice hotel in Korea, I was impressed with just about everything, with the exception of the hotel plumbing. I pulled back the shower curtain and noticed that my first shower here was going to be interesting. I'm only 6 feet tall, still my head touched the ceiling of the shower stall, and the showerhead came to the middle of my chest. Plus, I was on the 30th floor, which meant there was very little water pressure, and it seemed like I almost had to coax the water out of the faucet.

In Japan I've stayed at a place where the bathroom was so small I almost had to stand in the hallway to use it. At this hotel, flipping a valve on the sink operated the shower. The shower/sink combination made me do some serious contemplating when I flushed the toilet and the shower began to flow. I spent the next couple of hours thinking about which direction the water traveled.

Sometimes you end up staying in a hotel where the walls are just too thin. There is nothing like being awakened at 4 a.m. by the sounds coming from the room next door. Especially when it sounds like the person in the room is peeing from atop a 10-story building.

Swing Kit?

When I checked into my hotel in Taiwan, I found this in my bathroom (below). I opened it to see what a **"Swing Kit"** actually was.

I expected to see a condom or some kind of lubricant, but instead, found this:

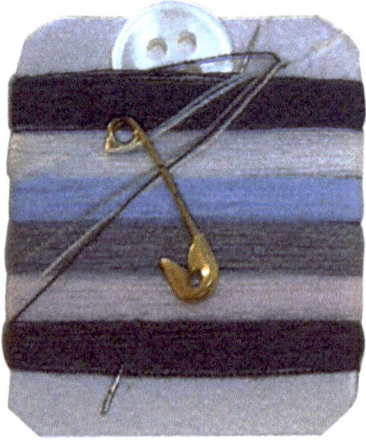

Do Not Disturb

I finally figured out the Do Not Disturb signs in Japan. On one side, "DO NOT DISTURB" is written in English. On the other side is something written in Japanese that I assumed said the same thing. I was wrong.

When I put the sign on my doorknob with the Japanese writing facing out, I'm quite certain it tells the cleaning crew I had a hard week and I need some rest. Therefore, bang your broom handle against the wall and turn the loudspeaker on your vacuum to FULL VOLUME. Then, yell in Japanese to the other end of the hall that you need window cleaner. After that, get your cleaning cart moving as fast as you can and ram it into my door.

I've also noticed if I leave the Do Not Disturb sign on my door past noon, I receive a phone call from housekeeping telling me I have a Do Not Disturb sign on my door.

A Room with a View?

I convinced my girlfriend, Holly, to come along with me on a trip to Singapore. I wanted everything to be perfect, so I did something I rarely do when I travel for business — *I PLANNED*. I had my travel agent book an upper level room with a king-sized bed at one of Singapore's finer five star hotels, which is a 70-story building.

After our 23-hour flight followed by a 30-minute cab ride, we were more than ready to check in. I presented myself to the desk clerk and she typed in my name. Five minutes passed and she looked up from the screen and asked for my confirmation number.

This isn't what you want to hear as you stand in the lobby with "airplane hair" knowing that you have about 30 minutes left on your 24-hour deodorant. As I handed her my confirmation number, she said I didn't seem to be in their computer. I explained that prior to leaving Phoenix, I'd confirmed my room directly with the hotel and I didn't understand what the problem was.

At that point, the clerk excused herself and went into the back room. (The back room is where they always go when they realize they've screwed up.) There must be a book of excuses back there that tells them how to explain why someone's room isn't available.

When she returned, the excuse she had selected was probably the dumbest excuse since the creation of "the dog ate my homework." She looked at me with total seriousness as she said, "Your room is only confirmed based on availability at the time of your arrival."

If it hadn't been happening to me, I would've laughed pretty hard at that statement. Instead, I made it clear I was not amused and firmly said, "I WANT TO TALK TO YOUR MANAGER. NOW!"

The clerk again excused herself and returned to the back room. (The back room is also where they keep an off-duty cleaning lady who impersonates the hotel manager when needed.) The person who came from the back room politely greeted us and tried to help by offering a substitution.

Instead of us being on an upper level floor, they were going to put us on the 27th floor. "This room comes with a beautiful view of the harbor," she informed us. However, because you now have a beautiful view of the harbor, your guaranteed room rate will increase $20 dollars per night." Then, for that extra touch of Singapore service, they told me I couldn't have a king-sized bed; I'd have to settle for a room with two queen beds. It's now 1 a.m., my deodorant has expired, and all we wanted to do was go to sleep.

We got to our room and the first thing I noticed was the queen beds were actually doubles. Knowing I was paying an extra $20 a night for a spectacular view, I opened the curtains to see how this hotel defines a beautiful view of the harbor. My breath was taken away, and I couldn't believe my eyes. It was spectacular! It was the most beautiful construction site I'd ever seen. There were cranes and steel girders, cement barriers and yes, even jackhammers. It would bring a tear to the eye of a construction worker. However, I'm a teacher and not a construction worker and didn't find this view even the slightest bit romantic.

It was now officially time to complain, so I called Saskia, my travel agent, and repeated the events of the last hour. Even though I knew that none of this was her fault, I asked her to call hotel management and try to take care of this matter for me immediately. After that, we went to bed.

Saskia was my "Princess in Shining Armor!" About an hour after our discussion, I was awakened by a call from the real hotel manager. She was apologetic and told me everything would be taken care of in the morning.

She kept her word, and we were moved to a business room on the 60th floor. We had a king-sized bed that covered two time zones. This time, there was a better view of the harbor and they lowered my per-night rate to less than my original guaranteed rate.

Thank you Saskia for making the rest of the trip a pleasant one!

Another Point of View

When I was checking in at one of the nicer hotels in Taiwan, the receptionist asked me if I would prefer a lakeside view or a city street view. I thought about my options for almost a full second. What options? This was a slam-dunk. I told the lady that a lakeside view would be perfect.

I got to my room and opened the curtains to see my view of the lake. Once again, reality did not meet expectations. There was a lake, and if you looked real hard you could see the sun reflect off of it way out in the distance. What the receptionist neglected to tell me was that in between the lake and the hotel was probably one of the biggest landfills in Taiwan.

Room 911

I flew from Korea to Malaysia and arrived late one evening. I got there one day before my boss was supposed to arrive. I chuckled at the fact that my assigned room number was 911. I checked out my surroundings and saw I had a small body of water just outside my window. At that time, I didn't think much about it.

I was in the bathroom brushing my teeth when it became obvious that three or four mosquitoes were extremely interested in sharing the room with me. After a couple of well-calculated snaps of a towel, the room occupancy count was back down to one.

It'd been a long day, so I climbed into bed. I usually sleep in a pair of boxers and lay on top of the covers. Not more than 10 minutes after lights out, the terror began. In honor of their fallen buddies, a new squadron of mosquitoes decided they needed to do a fly-by and buzzed my ears. I got up, turned on the light, grabbed my "mosquito-snapping towel," and went hunting. Fifteen minutes later, I was convinced I'd eliminated all of them. This time, I grabbed a shirt with a hood for more protection, turned off the lights, and got back into bed.

At 1 a.m., I felt the bite of a mosquito on the top of my foot. Once again I got up, turned on the light and grabbed my towel. I saw more of them flying around the ceiling light fixture. I snapped my towel at them and ended up hitting the globe that fit around the light, knocking it off. The globe hit the floor and shattered. It took me about five more minutes to get this batch of mosquitoes killed. Once more, I proved my superiority over those dumb bugs.

I'm sure I was quite a sight as I bounced around the room in my boxers and hooded shirt, swinging a towel. I discovered the bloodsuckers were coming into my room from the pond outside my window, via an air vent that couldn't be closed.

This time before getting back in bed, I put on a pair of sweat pants and got under the covers. I laid there for a couple of minutes, knowing there was no way a stupid mosquito was going to get me now. *Is this going to be my ritual for the next six weeks?* I thought hopelessly.

It took no time for me to answer that question. I got dressed, packed my bags, and went down to the reception desk. I briefly described my recent gymnastics program and demanded a new room. Their immediate reply was there were no vacancies and they couldn't move me. I told them, "Fine, I'll go to another hotel!"

As I began going through the yellow pages in front of them, they looked at my reservation and saw that I was supposed to be there for six weeks. All of a sudden, a room became magically available. I went to my new room, there were no mosquitoes, and I was happy.

The next day, my boss showed up right on schedule. She checked in, and we met for lunch. I asked her what her room number was and she replied 911. Then she added, "It has a pretty fish pond just outside the window." I smiled.

The Other Room 911

Unlike the preceding story about Room 911, which took place before the horrendous events on 9/11/01, this happened after that fateful day, giving the room number a new, more sinister meaning.

This time, the location was Singapore and I was in the process of checking into my hotel after traveling 28 hours from Phoenix.

I was going through the all too familiar process of checking in at 1 a.m. and the receptionist greeted me and asked me if I had a nice flight. She saw I was a frequent guest, and welcomed me back to the hotel. She looked at my reservation and noted I would be checking out in three days.

I showed her my copy of the reservation, which had been faxed to me from the hotel's reservation desk. It clearly stated I'd be checking out after 10 days, not three. She apologized for their mistake, but then informed me they wouldn't be able to accommodate me after three days.

I immediately asked for the manager. He came out and I explained the situation. He and the receptionist went into "the back room." The receptionist reappeared about five minutes later and told me that they would have a room for me as scheduled.

She began to book my room and said, "Mr. Blanton, you have reserved a king-sized bed on a non-smoking. Is this correct?"

I replied, "Yes."

She then looked at me and started her next sentence with the word "Because." I've learned that in Asia, when a sentence starts with that word, whatever follows isn't going to be good. She proceeded to tell me that *because* I was staying longer than originally planned by their screw up, the only room available was one with two single beds on a smoking floor.

After dropping this bomb on me, she looked me straight in the eyes and asked, "Will this be okay?"

My reply was short, sweet, and to the point. "No!"

She paused for a moment and then wanted to know why I didn't want the single bed on a smoking floor. I chose not to answer her and just pointed to the door to the "back room" and she knew the procedure from that point.

The manager again emerged from the great beyond; this time with breadcrumbs stuck to his face, which made having a serious conversation with him a little difficult. I explained to him I preferred not to spend the next 10 nights in a single Asian bed on a smoking floor. I once again reminded him that I didn't make any mistakes regarding the reservation, but if he preferred I would be willing to take my business and money elsewhere.

He told me it wouldn't be necessary for me to leave and he would see what he could do. The time was then 1:30 a.m. and the manager asked me to sit in the lobby for a while. A few minutes later the receptionist came back and told me that a guest had just checked out and I could have that room as soon as housekeeping cleaned it.

Finally, the time came to complete the check-in process. The receptionist asked for my credit card and faster than you can say, "…they all lived happily ever after," she informed me that my corporate card was rejected. I told her no problem, our finance department probably hadn't caught up with my expense reports, so I handed her my backup corporate card.

Before I could get the first card back into my wallet, she told me my second card was also declined. There is nothing more embarrassing than being told in front of everyone in line that your credit is no good. In front of an audience of ten people, I now had to call work and beg our finance department to make the payment so I didn't have to sleep in the park.

After the phone call, I decided to use my personal credit card, which went through with no problem. We were almost done and now the only thing preventing me from taking a shower and going to bed was getting a room key. The receptionist handed me a key and apologized that the room number was 911. I didn't think much of it. Actually, I thought it was kind of funny.

Finally, I made it to my room. The first order of business was to take a shower and wash away what was now 30 hours of travel. I got in the shower, the warm water was feeling pretty good, and then the curse began. All of a sudden, the showerhead flew off the wall, hit me on the chin, and landed on my little toe, which was incredibly painful.

The next evening, I went to dinner with our technical engineer, Lee Sipler. After dinner, Lee and I went to the men's room (no, this was not some type of male bonding activity). While I was at the urinal, I decided, for some reason, to look down. Not realizing the wall had a ledge on it, I moved my head down and promptly smashed it onto the corner of the ledge. This opened up a two-inch gash on my forehead.

Lee, who was standing about three feet to my right, heard the "thud," and started to laugh. He told me, "You should've seen the look on your face — it was priceless." Lee's a true friend.

I quickly completed the purpose of my men's room visit. I had a steady flow of blood dripping from my forehead at this point, so I tried to find something to use as a bandage.

This restroom was typical of many Asian restrooms; if you need tissue paper, you must buy it from a dispenser before you start your business. I had no coins with me, but fortunately Lee did. We got about five feet of toilet paper, and Lee folded it and handed it to me. Now, he and I had to walk the streets of Singapore with me holding bloody toilet tissue to my forehead. The curse of Room 911 had struck again.

I'm not superstitious, because it's bad luck to be superstitious, but I was beginning to believe this room was truly bad luck. When I charged food to my room, I was asked for my room number. When I replied with 9-1-1, the staff did a double take and their eyes got big.

After being in this room only four days, the staff began greeting me as I entered the hotel restaurant and lobby bar by saying, "Good evening, Mr. 911," followed by a couple of snickers and a smile.

After the fifth day, when asked my room number I simply replied, "Nine hundred and eleven."

Beachfront Property

During a rather long stay in the Philippines, my host, JoJo, scheduled a weekend on the beach just north of Manila. He told me that he was able to rent a cottage right on the beach. Early Saturday morning, he picked me up at my hotel and told me that his best friend and his wife would also be joining us.

Getting to the beach would require a three-hour drive. I was unaware that there is an unwritten law stating you must stop for food at least four times when traveling for three hours. It must be a law, because that's exactly what we did. About every 40 minutes, we stopped for rice, rice or fish, rice and fish, and finally rice, fish, and more rice.

During the drive up and in between bowls of rice, I thought it was pretty cool that we could get a three-bedroom cottage on the beach. What I was about to learn was my definition of cottage and JoJo's were at opposite ends of the spectrum. It turned out that the "cottage" was an open-air patio above a restaurant that was on the beach.

It was a single room with one double bed in the middle of it. In one corner of the room was a toilet. For privacy, there was a four-foot by four-foot piece of plywood to be held in front of you while you took care of business on the toilet. The other plumbing consisted of a hose that was attached to a faucet in the restaurant and run up along the wall.

I thought that the accommodations were funny and I didn't make a big deal about it. It was now about noon, so it was time to hit the water. First however, we had to have rice. After eating, we went down to the beach and rented a large log raft. It consisted of about 20 tree trunks wired together, and included a bench and some shade. Best of all, it also had an ice chest full of cold beer.

The way the beach rafts worked was a pretty good idea. The people you rent the raft from take you out about a quarter mile and anchor you at that spot. When you're ready to come back in, you just stick a red flag on the front of the raft and they come get you. In the meantime, people would come out to us selling fish, rice, rice or fish, rice and fish, and not to mention rice, fish, and more rice. We stayed on the raft, snorkeled, and relaxed until sunset.

After getting back to land, we went into the restaurant to eat. We had chicken with no rice! Jokingly I said, "What, no rice?" All of a sudden a big bowl of rice was put in front of me.

After dinner, we went back to our cottage and the following thought occurred to me, *There are four of us and one double bed.* My friends actually thought we could all sleep together. Many options went through my head, but none of them involved sleeping with two other guys and a woman on the same bed.

So, I decided I'd sleep on the floor. As I was getting ready to lie down, I noticed that the floor was covered with ants. Change of plans! I opted to sleep on a wooden table that was in the corner, opposite the toilet.

I actually slept really well until I was awakened around 6 a.m. by a noise and a "fowl" smell. When I opened my eyes, the last thing I expected to see was a rooster sharing the table with me. Needless to say, I was a bit startled.

I ended up going outside and sitting on the beach to watch the sunrise. There was something about watching this magnificent sunrise that made the cottage, the rooster, and the rice all worthwhile. The colors that painted the sky made this one of the most spectacular sunrises I have ever seen.

Beautiful Mountains

There was one summer when Holly and I and another couple, John and Diane, went to Puerto Vallarta for a mini vacation. We were able to stay in a nice condo with a back yard patio that looked right out to the ocean and offered a spectacular panoramic view.

After taking in an evening that included local cuisine, margaritas and beer, we managed to find our way back to the condo to retire for the evening. I woke up around 5 a.m., went into the kitchen and started a pot of coffee.

Not long after that, Diane wandered into the kitchen, poured herself a cup of coffee and then we both head out to the patio to enjoy the view.

As we sat there, we started talking about the view and how perfectly shaped the mountains off in the distance were. It didn't dawn on either of us that there were no mountains off in the distance when we arrived the day before.

Speaking of dawn, the sun was beginning to rise from behind us and almost instantly Diane and I both realized that the perfectly shaped mountains we'd been admiring were actually some closed patio umbrellas sitting slightly below and about five feet in front of us.

Our "special" mountains

The Suite

I had to go to San Jose, California to work a Semiconductor show. Being that San Jose is where I grew up, I invited my girlfriend, Holly, and our friends, John and Diane, to join me. Our plan was to get a hotel for the weekend, they would leave on Sunday and then I would check into my pre-arranged hotel for the show. When we got to our "weekend" room, we discovered there was one king-sized bed and a couch. The couch was not a sleeper/sofa and even though John and Diane are good friends, they were not good enough friends to share a bed with.

I ended up going to the front desk to correct our sleeping arrangements. They did not have another room with two beds as originally reserved, so they moved us to a mini-suite with a sleeper/sofa, which was more room, but the four of us had to share one bathroom that was located inside the suite bedroom.

The bathroom location was somewhat inconvenient and we now had to factor the bathroom into our scheduling when preparing to go out for the evening. This bathroom was barely equipped to handle the two shaving kits belonging to John and me, but the semi-truck load of feminine products that the ladies brought kind of pushed it over the edge. Even with all of this, the four of us got through the weekend and still remained friends.

On Sunday we were getting ready to check out and I was going through the room to make sure nothing was left behind. I opened a closet door and then called for John to come to where I was. We looked into the closet to see that the "closet" was actually a second bathroom. Because of the location of that particular door, the four of us never opened it and just assumed for the better part of two days that the door led to a closet.

Alarm Clocks

I think of myself as a fairly intelligent person. I can program my digital clock so it doesn't continuously flash 12 o'clock, 24 hours a day. However, for some unexplainable reason, alarm clocks with two alarm features always get the best of me.

I was in Brookfield, Connecticut ending a six-day trip. I had an early flight home in the morning, so before going to bed I set the alarm for 6 a.m. as a precaution, just in case I overslept. I got into bed and the next thing I knew, the buzzer woke me. I thought I'd set the alarm for music, but I didn't dwell on it much.

I took my shower, gathered my belongings, and checked the room just to make sure I wasn't leaving anything behind. The whole time I did these things, I failed to make the connection that even though I had been getting out of bed at the same time for the previous 5 days, for some reason on that particular day, it was still dark outside.

I went down stairs to checkout. I asked the lady behind the desk to arrange for transportation to take me to the bus stop where I'd catch a shuttle to the airport. About 15 minutes later, my taxi arrived. As we were putting my suitcase into the trunk, the driver told me that the terminal didn't open until 4 a.m.

I heard what he said, but I guess I didn't understand what he was actually trying to tell me. About 5 minutes into the cab ride, he asked me what I was going to do until the terminal opened. My response was, "I thought you said the terminal opened at 4 a.m."

His response was, "What time do you think it is?"

At that moment, I looked at my watch for the first time since shutting off my alarm. My watch read 1:20 a.m. I looked at his dashboard and that clock also read 1:20 a.m.

Realizing I was now in the running for dumbest man on the planet, I had the driver drop me off at an all-night restaurant near the bus stop. I had breakfast and several cups of coffee.

Around 2:30 a.m., I noticed a gentleman sitting on the other side of the dining area with his two suitcases and a computer case. As much as I really wanted to know if I was truly the dumbest man on the planet or if I had competition, I felt some things are simply better left alone.

The Wake Up Call

I've heard many humorous stories regarding wake up calls. Knowing that these stories always happen to someone else is what makes them so funny.

I'm such a light sleeper (during the night I can hear insects breathe), I have no problem responding to an alarm or wake up call. Whenever I schedule a wake-up call, I also set a travel alarm that accompanies me on my trips. The alarm acts as my snooze alarm.

The hotel that I was staying at in Singapore delivered my morning calls promptly each day for the entire three weeks of my stay. So, on the final night of this trip, I didn't set my snooze alarm. I was excited about finally going home, so I figured there would be no reason to snooze. Since the hotel hadn't missed a wake-up call yet, I felt I could rely on that call to get me going.

Well it finally happened, after 17 years I actually put my trust in the hotel wake-up call. On the morning I was supposed to leave Singapore (notice the word "supposed"), guess what didn't happen.

Correct! My 5:45 a.m. wake-up call didn't happen. I woke up at 7:30 when I heard the wake-up call in the room next door. Knowing it's a 20-minute ride to the airport and that my flight would be leaving in 10 minutes, there was only one thing I could do.

I said some very bad words, and when I was done I said them all again. Then, I called the front desk and said some more very bad words. Shortly after my little tirade, the manager called me back and guess what, I found some more bad words that I hadn't even used yet. He claimed their computer showed that the call was delivered, but I begged to differ.

I rescheduled my flight for the next day and scheduled another wake up call. Later on, I set the room alarm, I set my watch alarm, I also set my computer alarm, as well as the one for my pocket planner. If I missed my flight the next day, the reason would be because I was too busy turning off all of my alarms.

Since I had some bonus free time on my hands, I decided to stay in my room and review some work documents for the remainder of the day. While I was sitting at the desk, the phone rang. I answered the phone and on the other end was the recorded voice of a very perky Asian woman, wishing me to have a very nice day. It was my wake-up call exactly 12 hours after it should have happened. I felt the need for some more bad words.

What the #%@$?

I've traveled for many years and I am to the point where I've seen many things; some cute, some strange, and some that just made me say, "What the #%@$?"

I had a two-week assignment in Oregon. I elected to stay at one of my favorite hotels in a city named Tigard. While I was there, I learned that construction, spring break, and Easter should never, under any circumstances, be combined when making a hotel reservation for business.

As I checked in for the start of my two-week stay, the desk clerk was open and honest about their construction project, which was to begin the following morning. She warned me that there would be noise, including jackhammers.

I knew I could endure the inconveniences that come with construction, especially since I encounter that all the time. I told the clerk it probably wouldn't be too bad and I made the decision to stay at this hotel instead of going out and trying to find another one.

What she didn't tell me was the hotel was already "infested" with kids and their parents on a spring break holiday.

After checking in, I went to the elevator so that I could get to my room on the eighth floor. When the elevator doors opened, I was a bit surprised to be greeted by six teenaged girls stacked in a pyramid. I decided to wait for the second elevator.

When the next set of doors opened, I was face to face with three luggage dollies being used as go-carts by some young boys. They came flying out of the elevator, forcing me to quickly move aside so I wouldn't become hotel lobby "road kill."

I finally got to my room, unloaded my stuff and headed downstairs for a quick lunch. When the elevator doors opened on the eighth floor, a boy quickly walked out. As I went to push the "Lobby" button, I noticed it as well as the buttons for floors one through seven had already been pushed.

When I stopped on the seventh floor, a man got on and he noticed that all of the buttons from our current floor to the lobby had been pushed. He looked at me and all of a sudden I felt like I owed him an explanation. We both got out on the sixth floor to take a different elevator.

When that one came, we got in only to discover that all of the buttons on this elevator had also been pushed. He looked at me and said, "This is going to be a long week."

One of the main reasons I prefer to stay at this particular hotel is because they have a nice Jacuzzi and workout room that I like to use after ending my workday. During my two-week stay, I never once got to work out or use the Jacuzzi because no matter what time I went, there were so many kids playing around that it looked like recess at an elementary school.

Another reason I always choose this hotel is because they offer a great breakfast buffet and a decent happy hour. One morning, I went down for my breakfast and a family of four had walked in just ahead of me. As I stood in line behind the family, the father lifted the lid from the serving tray to show his young son the scrambled eggs.

It would have been nice to see "Dad" scoop out some eggs and put them on his son's tray. Instead, the son decided it would be a great time to clear his throat and cough for about five seconds while looking directly into the egg tray. Needless to say, breakfast ended for me at that moment.

Due to the construction, they had to keep moving the "Managers Reception Happy Hour" to various rooms. This was kind of interesting because it turned into a game of hide and seek with cocktails. They kept changing the venues because of noise, dust, or available space. If I was lucky enough to find that day's mystery location, I was rewarded with free beer.

The hotel was also planning a big Easter Sunday brunch. In order to accommodate the large number of people they were expecting to attend, they had to move Sunday's breakfast buffet to its third location in as many days. They threw some tables in a room, and put tablecloths on the tables to give them a semi-formal appearance. The well-decorated tables did not hide the fact that you'd still be forced to sit with strangers while you ate.

Early Sunday morning, I went downstairs around 7:30 a.m. in an attempt to elude the crowd and their kids. I found an empty table in the corner, and sat down to eat my breakfast. Soon after I sat down, two families came to my table and asked if they could join me. They consisted of five adults, six children, three dolls, a toy truck, and a talking cow.

It took almost a whole minute before one of the kids had spilled his milk. Immediately the boy's mother scolded him and he started crying. Picture this: as I sat there trying to eat my Easter breakfast, two busboys were trying to change our milk soaked table linens while a bunch of people tried to help them, plus there was a screaming kid, an upset mother, and as if that wasn't bad enough, we had a wet talking cow.

Sometimes, you've just got to say, "What the #%@$?"

Only the Strong Survive

I was on my first trip to Paris, and after a confusing 90-minute attempt to exit the Charles De Gaulle International Airport, I arrived at my hotel with most of my sanity still intact.

As I walked into the lobby, a disturbing sight brought me to a total standstill. The last thing I expected to encounter in France was roughly 200 Chinese vacationers who'd just arrived and were checking in ahead of me. I knew at that very moment that my stay *would not* be as the hotel name implied, a "Great Holiday."

After my second day at the hotel, it seemed my worst fears weren't going to materialize. Aside from checking in, I didn't see any signs of the Asian army that had arrived a couple of days earlier. The hotel wasn't large, and I wondered where 200 Chinese people could be hiding.

Monday morning my curiosity was put to rest.

It was now a painful fact that my most frustrating experiences at hotels occur during the breakfast buffet. My trip to France was no exception. The Chinese delegation was about to checkout of the hotel, but first they had a buffet to conquer.

As soon as I walked into the restaurant, there were people piled up everywhere. Little did I know I was about to experience the most chaotic meal of my life. I was able to locate a table, and I set my coffee down to mark my territory, then headed for the buffet line.

Through my many years of travel, I've stood in numerous breakfast lines at various hotels. During those times, I can't think of a single instance where I felt the need to hold my suitcase as I gathered my scrambled eggs. Unfortunately, there were at least 10 of the vacationers who did not share my feelings about "Breakfast Baggage."

I've never taken a class titled Breakfast Buffet 101, but I've always thought the food line begins where the plates are located. Once again, my logic did not apply in this situation. It was obviously going to be the "Law of the Jungle" if I wanted to eat.

After having my shins smashed with luggage, literally being forced out of line a couple of times, and waiting for breakfast items to be refilled, I was finally able to get enough food on my plate so I could return to my table.

Shortly after sitting down, one of the vacationers carrying a plate of food resembling a small mountain decided he was going to join me at my table. I had no say in the matter.

After he sat down, I noticed he had a mole that looked like a small finger sticking out of the side of his nose. Growing out of that "finger" was one four-inch hair. From that moment on, I couldn't stop staring at "The Mole" and thinking about the Austin Powers "moley, moley, moley" scene.

Not long after he sat down, his mountain of food was gone, but I was barely halfway done with mine. During his "Feeding Frenzy," he produced sounds I'd never heard come from any human being. As an added bonus, as if I wasn't able to see what was on his plate, he gave me ample viewing time to see the food inside his mouth as he chewed.

I patiently sat through the view of the mole, the hair, the noises, and watching the early stages of digestion without getting upset or sick. My patience finally came to an end when he pulled out a cigarette. Anybody who knows me knows exactly how I feel about cigarette smoke while I eat.

I put my hands together and said, "Please, no smoke." He looked directly at me, shook his head no, lit the cigarette, and then took a long drag from it. Shortly after his initial puff, he went to tap his cigarette in the ashtray. As soon as his hand was within reach, I took the cigarette from him and put it out. I then gave him the "Bring-it-On" motion. He just stared at me. I didn't know if he was going to cry or fight me, but I definitely surprised him.

As he sat there, I stared directly into his eyes (but I still saw the mole). He finally responded by getting up and leaving. This was the first time I've ever done anything like that and I hope I never do it again. It did, however, remind me of two useful words for the future: Room Service.

TELEVISION

"...I checked back later only to find nude co-ed Ping-Pong."

What's On TV?

When I travel to the same places over and over, there eventually comes a time when sightseeing, shopping, or going out and getting lost no longer appeals to me. When I reach that level, there are only a few things left for me to do. That usually means I end up watching TV at the hotel.

During my years of travel, I've noticed the following characteristics of international television. No matter what country you're in, each has a particular trait when it comes to soap operas. As we all know, American soaps always involve a story line where someone's having an affair. Once the affair turns into true love, one of the involved parties develops an incurable disease. While the one with the disease is in the hospital being treated, the other falls in love with the doctor and then the cycle repeats itself.

In Japan, many of the soap operas I encountered were about crime. When a crime is committed on a Japanese soap, there are a lot of stares and glares accompanied by sharp musical sounds, but no words. These soaps almost always end with someone crying and running hysterically through the streets until a passing car strikes them.

Soap operas from India also have a common theme and try to emulate, *West Side Story*. At any second, the entire cast will break into song and dance over the simplest things. For example, a man at an airport is buying a ticket and suddenly he's standing on top of a pile of luggage singing. Or a young couple in a taxi starts singing, only to have the taxi driver join them in perfect harmony.

Heavyweight TV

No matter how bored I get, I will never become a big fan of soap operas. My desire to find televised sports that I'm familiar with has caused me to wear out many hotel remotes. In Japan, you'll find two or three channels dedicated to Sumo Wrestling.

Sumo Wrestling is where huge people try to push and shove each other out of a very small space in their quest to earn a piece of cloth as a trophy. We have this same event in the US, only we call it the Spring White Sale at Macy's.

Sumo Wrestling can be interesting to watch because of the tradition and pride that accompanies the sport. However, the one tradition I can do without is the close-ups of the participants from behind.

Take Me Out to the Ball Game

Asian baseball is an experience you must witness to truly appreciate. In the US, you go to a game, buy a hotdog and beer, then sit until something good happens so you can stand up and cheer. In Asia, fans enter the stadium with a wide variety of noisemakers like drums, cymbals, bells, horns, whistles, clappers, and screaming children. From the first pitch to the last out, it's continuous and well-organized high-volume noise and chanting. I'm sure many of the fans go home more exhausted than the guys who actually played the game.

When the games are televised, it's difficult to understand the announcers because of the background noise. Not knowing the languages doesn't help me, either.

This Game Was a Real Barn-Burner

Many times you'll find a little less than semiprofessional basketball games on television when traveling abroad. These games usually feature something like the local beer company against the local automotive retailer.

I was in the Philippines watching one such game from my hotel. I had a total blast listening to both of the play-by-play announcers totally destroy American slang. At one point in the game, one player collided with another causing one of the men to hit the floor extremely hard. The announcers' play-by-play call was, "Wow! He really got 'knocked up' by the other team."

During this same game, the stadium they were playing in caught fire. Everyone evacuated the building and they just left the cameras running until eventually the power went out. It was kind of weird to watch a fire from the inside.

The Sports Channel

When I went to Switzerland on a business trip, I got my first experience with American versus European television programming.

After 16 hours of travel, I finally made it to the hotel. I arrived the same day the world governments were preparing for the G8 Summit, which would take place a few miles away in France. Due to heavy protesting by many of the locals, I opted to stay at the hotel instead of going downtown, since it had been the center of some violent activities.

I decided I should just order room service and go to bed. As I lay in bed, I decided to watch some television before falling asleep. I found the Swiss equivalent to ESPN.

When I fell asleep I was watching track and field on Channel 20. Sunday morning, I woke around 5 a.m., turned on the TV, and immediately went to Channel 20 for some more sports. This time there were no sports; instead a nude woman was sitting on a motorcycle talking about dirt bike racing. This got my attention real quick.

When I checked that channel a little later, there were three women bowling in the nude. The three looked like a family. There was daughter (around 20-ish), mom, and grandma. Daughter looked good, mother looked like a truck driver, and grandma … we won't go there. (I just thank God that I hadn't eaten breakfast yet.)

I checked back later only to find nude co-ed Ping-Pong. At 6 a.m., I went upstairs to work out then I had breakfast. When I returned to my room, I checked Channel 20 again. I think it had reverted back to normal programming because it was showing Grand Prix motor racing and I'm pretty sure the drivers were all wearing clothes.

KTV

No matter where you go in Asia, the plain fact is you'll see miles and miles of signs on buildings. These are billboards most Americans can't read. However, among all the foreign characters on these signs, you'll notice three letters written in English that stand out like a Sumo Wrestler in a ballet class.

These letters for most Asians mean fun, friendship, and drinking. For me, they spell out fear, anxiety, embarrassment, and drinking.

Time Zones, Beer & Left-Handed Chopsticks

The letters I'm referring to are KTV, which is universally known as Karaoke Television.

The sole purpose of the karaoke nightclub is to allow people to celebrate special occasions or to gather after a hard day's work and let off steam by singing. The thing is, I didn't take choir in school. I played in a band, but I was not allowed to use a microphone. If I start to sing in my car, a policeman will show up out of nowhere and signal me to "knock it off." My singing could do more damage and spread more fear than Frankenstein, King Kong, and Godzilla combined. Simply put, I'm a bad singer.

My host usually ends up asking me what form of entertainment I would like for the evening when we go out. If I reply, "Let's go to the cultural museum," we go to a KTV pub. If I ask to be taken to a shopping mall, we go to a KTV pub. If I say, "Let's go see pretty ladies," we go see pretty ladies, and then we go to a KTV pub.

Once inside one of these places, you're put into a small room with a big screen TV, some song books, a couple of microphones, and a waitress. I usually sit back and enjoy watching and listening as everyone else sings. After a couple of hours or a pitcher of beer, I'll get up enough nerve to attempt to sing. I figure I'm 10,000 miles from home and none of my friends will be able to hold it against me.

I usually have one co-worker with me when I'm at one of these pubs. Our engineer, Lee Sipler, and I will try to sing at least one song if we're out together, just because we want to be good guests. It's obvious that neither Lee nor I will be leaving our current jobs to pursue any type of singing career in the future.

There was one time that Lee and I actually sang a duet. Since then, we've both decided we won't force that kind of pain and suffering on anyone again and have cancelled our world karaoke tour. Lee and I also have a pact where we both agree not to discuss each other's singing with people we know.

In the KTV pubs, you're given catalogs containing hundreds of songs to choose from in a variety of different languages. There are a lot of English songs listed in the catalog; however the local people for some reason seem to think the only song an American knows and wants to sing is "Country Roads" by John Denver. They usually have the karaoke machine pre-programmed with this song to appear about four times an hour when Americans are present.

There was one time that sticks out as my most memorable Karaoke experience. One December, Lee and I were at a pub in Japan. We were sitting at the bar and I felt a light tapping on my leg. When I turned around, there was an 11-year-old girl standing there with her family (mom, dad, and grandparents).

I smiled at her and noticed that she had a microphone in her hand. She asked me in perfect English if I'd sing "Here Comes Santa Claus" with her. How could I refuse? I think it was probably my best singing effort too. When we were done, she gave me a sweet hug and her family shook my hand and thanked me for singing with their girl.

The Rules of the Game

I was sitting in a pub in Ireland watching a cricket match on television when I made a comment to a gentleman sitting next to me that I didn't understand the game. The man looked at me for a second and then said, "It's very much like your American baseball."

I replied with, "To me, baseball makes sense. I just don't understand this sport."

From that point on, the man spent a great deal of time trying to explain the rules of cricket to me. When we were done, the man told me he had only one question about baseball and asked if I could clear it up for him. "If a baseball hits the foul pole, why is it a fair ball?"

AIR TRAVEL

"...I don't want someone who can prepare my meal in a small room behind a curtain mad at me."

Time Zones

If you're easily confused or you think the International Date Line is a way to pick up "foreign dates" on the Internet, *do not* attempt to travel across many time zones on the same trip. For example, if you fly from Japan to San Francisco in a 24-hour period, you'll see two sunrises, two sunsets fly for 11 hours and arrive in San Francisco 4 hours before you left Japan.

Your body doesn't like it when you do this and it will attempt to get even with you. You'll find that at 3 a.m. you're suddenly wide-awake and the only things on TV are "infomercials" for stuff you'll never buy or a bunch of people who have never been fat a day in their life selling weight loss products.

Nothing but Class

When you book a flight, you're given various options for how you can travel. This may also be referred to as your desired comfort level. These levels are known as First Class, Business Class, or Economy. No phrase could be more truthful than the statement, "You get what you pay for," when flying. If you pay the extra money, you are taken care of very well. Whereas, if you opt for the cheap seats, you'll get there at the same time as the more expensive seats, but you'll feel like it took twice as long to get there.

For those of you who haven't had the opportunity to make the decision as to which class to choose, let me give you these simple guidelines:

First Class — This is like going through life, eating only desserts and never gaining weight. Or, it's like being allowed to go through the "Ten Items or Less" lane with two shopping carts full of groceries. First Class is located just outside the gates of heaven.

Business Class — This is usually nothing but a continuous happy hour. It can almost be compared to a major social event. Not only do you need a laptop computer to get in, but you also must take it out at least once and pretend to use it or watch a movie on it.

To sit in Business Class, you must be emotionally stable because you aren't judged by your job title, income, or even the amount of frequent flyer miles you've earned during the year. The fact is, your status is determined by the size of your monitor. You may feel inadequate if you look over and see the guy next to you has a bigger one in his lap than you. This could lead to a condition commonly known as PC Envy.

Economy Class — Best described as being stuck in a phone booth with six people in downtown Detroit during the winter. On a long flight, Economy Class has the same comfort as a "Mosh Pit" at a heavy metal concert. I haven't been able to prove this yet, but I think clocks actually run slower when you're seated in Economy Class.

You also receive good food service in First and Business Class. You get to choose from items on a menu and the food comes on real china. In Economy Class, they hand you a box that contains something resembling tree bark, an apple, a granola bar, and a breath mint.

Children on Airplanes

I feel sorry for parents who must fly with their small children. They immediately become social outcasts. It starts at the gate; they get that evil glare from other passengers, which translates to: "You better not be sitting anywhere near me."

Moving on to the boarding process, things get worse. Most flights allow two small carry-on items when you board. As we all know, traveling with a small child requires a utility vehicle full of baby equipment, the entire deli section from a local supermarket, and a rattle.

Now comes the next step, taking a seat. Upon seeing a parent holding a child (whose tee shirt should read: "Daddy's Little Monster"), every passenger with a vacant seat next to him repeats the same little prayer, "O God, please don't sit beside me."

Once airborne, the baby cries because that's what babies do. I have no problem with the crying, it's that high-pitched shrill noise they sometimes make, the one that can be heard by dogs on the ground, that drives me crazy.

The parents realize this sound is annoying to other passengers and begin to try to calm the baby. They go through a form of communication with the child that looks and sounds rather odd. In fact, if they weren't with the child and did this, they'd immediately be admitted to a mental hospital with no questions asked.

They start making faces and odd noises while turning their heads awkwardly, in an effort to entertain the child. This usually gets the baby to stop crying because he suddenly realizes the people making these funny faces and noises will one day represent him at the PTA.

Next, I can just see the baby thinking to himself, *Okay, I got the adults to look silly so now it's time for some* real *action.* At first he'll just lay there and smile. He knows that combination will set off a sensor all flight attendants have that tells them there is a happy, cute baby in seat 17B.

The flight attendants then come over make the same faces and noises, as well as touching his little cheeks, blowing him kisses and giving him a set of wings to show he was a happy flyer. They make such a big deal out of it that I wish I was one and a half feet tall, bald and had drool all over my face.

The Nightmare Finally Happens

During flights, kids have shown me that they want to be my special friend by putting carrots into my ear while I slept. I've had my hair pulled, my seat kicked, drinks dumped in my lap, and had a rattle hit me upside the face. Through all of this, I've usually kept my composure.

There was one time that will definitely go down as my flight from hell. Due to some events at work, I had to push my flight home from Singapore out one day. In doing this, I lost my seat in business class and had to fly home in economy. I was prepared to be somewhat uncomfortable, but since I was going home, I would just accept it. As I sat there, I felt pretty good and thought the trip home shouldn't be that bad. Unfortunately, that good feeling was about to come to an abrupt end. In the distance I could hear a kid screaming. It got louder and louder until finally I was face to face with the little Chinese sound machine. Standing beside me was a woman holding a baby that was screaming and wouldn't stop. She got in the seat beside me and had plans to hold the baby for the entire 13 hours.

It was a sold out flight, there were no seats in front of us and being that she was one of the last passengers to board, there was no convenient place to put her baby equipment. I looked at the woman, ready to say something like, "You can't be serious." However, looking into her eyes, I had a moment of compassion. Her face looked like she had just worked a 14-hour day and it was only 7 a.m. She said, "Baby cry all night." I tried to see if I could move so that she had a place to put her baby or, just try to escape the inevitable, but there were no available seats. The baby cried for about eight of the 13 hours. The mother kept apologizing and I just kept repeating it's okay. I even offered once to hold the baby so that the mother could eat her meal and rest. When she handed her son to me, he just looked at me and started to cry (I have the same effect on some adults).

Somehow, I managed to get through this ordeal, but before we landed in San Francisco, the child had grabbed my beard while I slept, pulled my hair while eating dinner, knocked his mother's drink into my lap, and kicked my breakfast into the aisle. As a special parting gesture, the kid decided to throw up on my shoulder an hour before landing.

Airplane 101

If I had the power to determine what courses were taught in schools, one I would require would be titled, "Airplane Etiquette and Common Sense." When certain people pass through the security checkpoints at airports, I believe the part of their brains that controls logic and common sense just shuts down.

For example, I'd never try to stuff everything I've ever owned into an overhead compartment. I've seen people out there who believe it's possible, though. There are also some people who read the sign that says "two carry-on bags per person" and actually think it's meant for everybody but them. Finally, if you're assigned a seat in the back of the plane, *do not* stow your carry-on items in the front of the plane as you board. This is rude and I will find you!

There are people who sit patiently for over an hour while waiting at the gate for their turn to board, then once they're on the plane, they decide now is a good time to go to the restroom. Doing this during the boarding process requires working your way up the aisle, against the flow of passengers trying to get to their seats. Airplane aisles are *not* wide enough for two people to pass. So, the restroom person coming causes a sort of dance with each person he or she attempts to pass.

When people arrive at the airport late, they never blame the taxi driver or the rental car agency for the delay. They never admit that even though their airplane has been taking off at the same time every day for the last two years, they can't plan their schedule well enough to get to the airport on time. Instead, they save all of their built up frustration for the person at the airline counter. In my opinion, this is probably the last person you'd want to tick off — they have the power to put you in the worst possible section of the plane.

Here is another basic rule: don't confuse your flight attendant with a waitress, waiter, or short order cook. They don't cook the food and aren't responsible for how it's made! They are given the responsibility of serving the meal (a TV dinner that was prepared while you were in high school) and hope that you'll still be friendly after you eat it. Most of the time, they're just as surprised as you are when they peel back the tinfoil cover prior to serving your meal. Airlines concentrate on travel, not catering. When I make my reservations for travel, it's never based on which airline serves the most flavorful steamed chicken patty.

The most brain cells lost while in flight award, in my opinion, is actually a tie. The first awardee was a woman on one of my flights from Phoenix to Denver who saw nothing wrong with changing her baby's diaper on the fold down tray in front of her. My other vote goes to a woman on a flight from Japan to San Francisco who went into the restroom barefoot. For those of you who don't understand the significance of this statement, the sticky floor is *not* to keep you from losing your balance...

I Can Hear You

Some travelers have a major misconception about the functional purpose of noise-canceling headsets. These headsets work by electronically eliminating background noise as you listen to music. This means a higher quality of sound for the listener.

Here is where some people have misunderstood how these items actually work. "Noise canceling" means the listener can't hear background noise. It *doesn't* mean it eliminates the noise coming from the person wearing the headset — this includes bad singing and certain body noises.

Calm Waters

The very first time I ever flew on a 747, I had a window seat. About an hour after we departed San Francisco for Manila, the pilot announced our position and gave us some flight details. I looked out the window and commented to the man sitting next to me about how smooth the ocean looked from 30,000 feet.

He looked out of the window, and then he looked at me and didn't say much. About an hour later, I made another comment about the smooth ocean waters, and he pretty much had the same response.

About 15 minutes after that, I looked through the window again and realized that I'd been looking at the wing of the aircraft, not the ocean.

I Smell Something Funny

Occasionally, actions with the best intentions will sometimes go "sour." When checking in for a recent flight, I was told that economy was sold out and I was automatically being upgraded to business class for the 11-hour flight. That was a good thing!

Once inside the airplane, I willingly traded seats with a lady so she could sit with her daughter. That too, was good. The man I ended up sitting next to had the worst case of gas known to mankind. That was very, very bad.

As we pushed back from the gate, the man fell asleep almost immediately. It was at that time the "evil spirits" started departing his body. For the first 30 minutes of the flight, everyone is confined to their seats, so I had to sit there and inhale what I thought was a mixture of sour milk, rotten eggs, and fish. Knowing that I couldn't just roll down a window, I prayed this man's gas would set off some sort of alarm and the overhead oxygen masks would be activated, but it never happened.

As soon as the fasten seat belt light went off, I bolted from my seat and went to stand with the flight attendants. They started talking about a foul stench coming from the middle of the plane in the upper deck. I told them it was the guy in the seat next to mine.

At first, they didn't believe that kind of a smell could come from a human being. I begged to differ. After about 20 minutes, they reached the same conclusion as me. The man in 15A had either just begun the early stages of decomposition, or he desperately needed to change his "Huggies."

Business class was packed, making it impossible for me to change seats. I prayed the fasten seat belt light would stay off for the entire flight.

One of the flight attendants, Jo Ann, finally decided it was time to take action. While this man slept, she sprayed some cheap raspberry perfume around the area near him. Then, she sliced an apple and put it on the console between "stinky" and my empty seat. The only thing this accomplished was to make the area smell like a fruit salad that had gone bad.

Later, she put two coffee bags between our seats. Once again, "old stinky" proved to be invincible. After two hours of fighting a losing battle, they decided to move me to first class for the remainder of the flight. I pity the person who sat in 15A on the next flight. Who knows what lingering odors remained in that seat!

The Great Escape

About once a year, I'm assigned a window seat for a long international flight. The way my luck runs, the person assigned to sit next to me is usually a large man who falls asleep immediately and snores loudly throughout the entire flight.

During a flight from Singapore to Los Angeles this particular seating arrangement was once again in play.

Shortly after takeoff, the man beside me began snoring something fierce. He slept through the bar service, the first meal, and dessert. Four hours into the flight, I needed to get out of my seat but I was trapped against the window and his body size kept me from making a clean exit.

I tapped the man politely but he didn't wake up. I tapped him a little harder and he still didn't wake up. I ended up pushing on his shoulder until he finally awakened. He looked at me like I'd just ruined the best dream he'd ever had. He mumbled a swear word or two and then got out of his seat so I could leave mine.

After a few minutes I returned to my seat. He got up with an attitude like he was doing me a big favor. At that moment it became real obvious we weren't going to form a long-lasting friendship. I sat down, and within 10 minutes he was once again snoring at high volume.

During the next few hours, I watched some movies and drank ice water. When one of the movies ended, many of the passengers started getting up to stretch their legs. I needed to do the same. However, once again I had to deal with getting around the human roadblock.

Not wanting to experience our previous encounter, I thought perhaps I could just climb over him. I thought about this for a moment and realized that the act itself would look like some kind of bizarre tribal mating ritual, so I decided I'd keep my dignity and come up with an alternate plan.

I looked at my cup of ice water for a moment and quickly the old myth of sticking someone's hand in water while they sleep came to mind. I didn't want to be that obvious so I came up with an idea I'm not very proud of, but I'd do it again if I ever get trapped in a window seat next to "Mr. Cranky."

I took an ice cube from my drink and lightly tossed it into the snoring man's lap. In about a minute, the ice cube had melted and seeped through his pants. He immediately sat straight up and bolted for the restroom. I was then able to get up and take a leisurely stroll to visit the restroom myself.

As I stated earlier, I'm not proud of this, but I believe it was Confucius who once said, "An ice cube on the pants is better than a burst bladder in the seat."

Wide Open Spaces

A myth I'd like to clear up involves the size of the restroom on an airplane. In the movies you get the impression the restroom is big enough to hold a small cocktail party or an aerobics class. This is *not* the case.

The restroom on most airplanes barely allows you enough space to turn around. If you have to sit down, you'll bang your head on the door and start grabbing for things to hold onto in order to aid your descent to the toilet. On the outside, it sounds like an aerobics class is taking place inside. That's probably how that whole myth got started.

It's Nice to Share

On a flight from Phoenix to Atlanta, my friend Karen was supposed to sit next to me, but she had to cancel at the last second. The man who ended up in her seat was big, to call him large would be like saying the *Titanic* had a small leak. As a matter of fact, if the *Titanic* wore pants, they would probably be the same size as this guy's. Thank you Karen!

I had to sit turned halfway in my seat to allow for this man's overflowing girth. In flight, he initiated the communication between us by asking me if I was going to eat my pretzels. I replied with a slight grunt and handed him my snack.

Later on, he spoke again. I guess he figured we'd bonded earlier when I gave him my pretzels. So, it was okay for him to ask me if I wanted the roll that came with breakfast.

Soon after that, the flight attendant came around and asked if we'd like refills on our coffee. The man beside me immediately blurted out, "I would!" With that, in what seemed like super slow motion, a piece of egg came flying out of his mouth and made a 9.9 landing in my coffee (it would have been a perfect 10.0 but it produced a small splash).

The flight attendant witnessed this incredible act of marksmanship. We both looked at each other and without missing a beat, she asked, "Would you like a *fresh cup* to go with your coffee?"

The Waiting List

Today, most businesses are doing everything they can to cut back on their travel expenses. In many cases, what this means to the business traveler is corporate travel guidelines now indicate Business Class tickets are no longer an acceptable means of travel.

When you're accustomed to flying in business class, an economy flight that's five hours or less is really nothing more than a minor inconvenience. However, when your itinerary indicates you'll be seated in an airplane for 10 to 20 hours, you no longer see this as an inconvenience — it's a matter of survival. Thus, you become willing to try just about anything to get upgraded into business class. The problem is, there are usually only four or five seats available for an upgrade and anywhere from 15 to 20 people who feel they should be awarded one of them.

After purchasing an economy fare ticket, the traveler must now hope his or her status in the airline's frequent flier program is high enough to use their coupons or miles to upgrade their current seating arrangements. Many people try to convince the person at the check-in counter they need to be upgraded by using some made up, stupid, or lame excuse. This pathetic type of begging just doesn't work, or at least it hasn't for me.

Normally you get put on a waiting list, which is just a few names smaller than the Los Angeles County phone directory. Then, you're told your name will be called if something becomes available. Approaching the gate with your wait list card in hand is like being on "Death Row" waiting for a call from the governor.

As you stand in a line with people who have the same grief stricken feeling, you can hear each of them ask the same question of the gate attendant as they reach the front of the line, "Are there any upgrade seats available yet?"

You hear the question being asked from as far back as five people. More importantly, from that same distance you can also hear the gate attendant's response, "Not yet, we'll call you if something becomes available." For some reason, you and the people in front of you feel the need to continue standing in line so you can ask the same question you just heard everyone else ask, only to get same response.

The wait list priority procedure is usually based on status, and the number of miles flown during a certain time. Bottom line, if you're not in the highest status category, your chances of winning the lottery are actually greater than being awarded an upgrade.

As your departure time gets closer, you and everyone else on the list are back in line to ask the next questions: Where am I ranked on the waiting list and what are my chances for an upgrade?

Now, it's time for the gate attendant to have some fun. After listening to excuses and the same question over and over, if the gate attendant sees that you don't have even the slightest chance for an upgrade, you'll get one of two responses:

In America, they'll look at you and start laughing. Then, the attendant will grab the person working with them at the counter and point to your position on the list. Then, they both start laughing, drop to the ground and continue laughing hysterically as they roll around on the carpet.

In Asia you'll get a little more respect. The gate attendant there will see that you don't have a chance for an upgrade and will politely respond, "There are just 387 people ahead of you. Please be seated and maybe something will be available soon."

The grumpiest people on an airplane are usually the ones who've lost their "elite" status for the first time, the next grumpiest are the ones who were too far down the waiting list to be upgraded. Being in economy class is definitely a step down.

If the person seated beside you was turned down for an upgrade, you can expect to hear every possible reason the person can come up with as to why he or she shouldn't be sitting next to you … for the entire flight.

So… That's Why He Didn't Eat His Meal

I came across this article in a Phoenix, Arizona newspaper. It speaks for itself.

FAA Probing Death on Express Flight

DES MOINES, IOWA — Officials are trying to determine whether a man who was dead on arrival at Des Moines International Airport died aboard the Express flight or before he boarded in Phoenix.

"We're satisfied that this passenger was alive when he boarded our aircraft," a spokeswoman for the Phoenix-based Express Airline said on Sunday. "We never would've allowed a passenger who had passed away to board an aircraft."

A report released by the Polk County medical examiner's office says the man's son told investigators he was "pretty much convinced he died in the airport terminal in Phoenix." The plane left the runway at 11:21 a.m. Saturday.

***Names have been intentionally removed from the above article.

Window or Aisle

As you know by now, seat assignment can make the difference between a comfortable and relaxing trip and wishing you were standing in line at the Department of Motor Vehicles rather than on the plane.

For business travelers, the most popular seat on an airplane is the aisle seat. Unlike the window seat where you're safely protected and have a wall you can rest against, the aisle seat is the airline version of audience participation. In the aisle seat, your head is a prime target to be banged by boarding passengers' carry-on luggage. In my experience, this baggage is never filled with clothing or pillows — it's usually books or power tools. The aisle seat also allows you to get up close and personal with the hairy bellybutton of a businessman as he stuffs his carry-ons into the overhead compartment above you.

The pleasurable encounters only happen in movies. I've never had a "Super Model" spend a few moments rearranging the overhead compartment above my seat — it is usually the "Wolf Man" or "Sasquatch."

In flight, the aisle seat offers other activities, like having your elbows smashed by out of control service carts, and getting up for the people sitting in the inside seats so they can use the restroom. These seatmates usually only feel the need when your tray is down and you're eating your meal. Or, when you're in the middle of working on a multi-page spreadsheet.

If there is a hell, it's the middle seat on an airplane. The person on either side of the middle seat is thus relegated to purgatory. For me, real hell would be to sit in a middle seat and be forced to watch the in-flight movies, which are all of the Brady Bunch sequels.

If you're in the middle, you have to strategically maneuver your elbows so that you have a place to rest at least one of them. You must keep one eye on each armrest, that way when the person beside you moves his arm, you can quickly thrust your elbow into the vacated spot and not move it until the plane has landed.

The Bulkhead Seat

For those of you unfamiliar with the bulkhead seat, it has a big wall right in front of it. Many times, the bulkhead wall is used to separate the various "Class" sections from each other. Many people see this wall as some sort of a vertical footstool, and I have some issues with that.

It always seems that when I travel, the people who have elected to use "the wall" as a footrest have some of the nastiest looking feet to ever walk this planet. I have no desire to look at someone's yellow, crusty, mangled toenails for a five-hour flight. This sight is even less appealing if you're having dinner in Economy Class and trying to eat the steamed chicken that comes with road tar gravy.

I think that when a person checks in for their flight, the person behind the counter should see if the passenger has a bulkhead seat. If the answer is yes, their next question should be, "May I see your feet?" If the person has feet that would get him or her barred from most zoos for life, an automatic seat reassignment should take place. That, or they should issue them some sort of high security socks that can only be removed by airport personnel once the passenger has reached his or her destination.

Let Me "Outta" Here

There is one other rule that people who seldom fly must learn and understand. If you are seated in row 37 of 40 rows, you *are not* going to be one of the first few people off the plane after it pulls up to the gate.

You won't be off of the plane in the first 10 minutes. Sit back and wait. You just spent 4 hours seated in an airplane. You can wait another 5 minutes so that you can get your carryon luggage in an orderly fashion. I've watched people seated at the window seat climb over two people to get to their bags; only to find that once they've grabbed their stuff, they can't move.

When the plane gets to the gate, "the ding" does not mean the start of a game called Airplane Twister.

It's Good to be Nice

My golden rule for flying is: "You *must* be nice to the flight attendants." My logic is simple. I don't want someone who prepares my meal in a small room behind a curtain to be mad at me.

This means don't push the call button unless you need something you can't take care of by yourself — like neutering a pet or informing the flight attendant that the person beside you has spontaneously combusted. I've been seated beside people who start pushing their call button before the plane is even in the air. For me, these people rate right up there with the people who run elevators in Asia.

This action truly does not make the flight attendants like you. I've been on enough flights to know that if a flight attendant wants to get even with you, they won't be vicious but they are incredibly creative.

Nice Pants

Shortly after boarding my flight to San Francisco from Korea, the man seated in the aisle seat across from me, Victor, got up and started taking pictures of the inside of the plane. He went into first class and it looked like a lightning storm from all the flashes. He even tried to get pictures of the flight attendants, but they were deep into their pre-flight routines. When he persisted and began to annoy them, he was promptly directed back to his seat.

During the flight, Victor downed four "airplane bottles" of whiskey before dinner, during dinner he had a couple more, and then he had one more following his dessert.

After the first movie ended, I got up to go stand near the galley and talk to the flight attendants and some other passengers who had gathered there. As I was talking to one of the flight attendants, we noticed Victor begin to slump forward until his face was pressed against the seat in front of him — he was passed out cold. The flight attendant, being the nice person she was, reclined his seat, leaned him back, put a pillow behind his head, and covered him with a blanket.

About an hour later, while I was talking to a flight attendant named Tracy, Victor came out of the restroom and walked directly between the two of us. As he returned to his seat, Tracy and I immediately noticed he was not wearing any pants. Tracy commented that in all her years of flying, this was a first.

Shortly afterwards, a passenger came up to Tracy to tell her that someone had left their pants and camera in the restroom. Tracy went in, got Victor's stuff, and put it on the floor in front of Victor's seat.

When Tracy came back I said, "You know, if you really wanted to have some fun, you could've held on to his pants and waited for him to ring his call button to ask if he had pants on when he boarded the plane". Almost immediately she went back, got the pants and put them in a cabinet in the galley.

I went back to my seat and watched another movie. When the movie ended, I got up to stretch my legs and ended up back in the galley talking with some of the other passengers. I looked up and noticed

Victor had joined us. He was standing there with a blanket wrapped around his waist.

We just stood there trying to hold back the snickers as Tracy walked up and asked Victor if he was cold. Victor said he was pretty sure he had pants on earlier, but he wasn't sure where he'd left them. Finally, after a long pause and a little laughter, Tracy gave him his pants back.

Just When You Think You've Seen it All

I was on a flight from Chicago, bound for Phoenix. We had just taxied to the start of the runway when a man sitting across the aisle and in front of me started to push his call button. The flight attendant motioned with his hands for the man to wait because we were getting ready to take off.

The pilot revved the engines and we started down the runway. We weren't off the ground 20 seconds when the man who'd been ringing his call button unbuckled his seatbelt and walked up to the flight attendant with his headphones in hand.

He tried to tell the flight attendant his headphones weren't working. The flight attendant let out a yell directed at this man telling him in no uncertain words, to get his butt back in his seat.

After we leveled off, the man started in with the flight attendant again by saying, "I want to know your name. You were very rude to me." He continued, saying that he'd sue the airline because they treat paying customers very badly.

The flight attendant stood in front of him and asked for his headphones. Then, he calmly told him, "I'm not going to give you another headset right now, I want you to sit and think for a moment about how dumb it was for you to do what you did."

With that, just about everyone seated in the general vicinity gave the flight attendant a big round of applause.

Why Do I Feel Rushed?

One summer morning I arrived at work around 7 a.m. At 8:15, my boss, Jay, walked into my office and told me I needed to leave for Israel immediately. Two and a half hours later, I was on my way to Israel via Canada.

During those two and a half hours, I had to book my flight, drive 17 miles home, pack, swing by my travel agent to pick up my tickets, and then drive 21 miles to the airport. Once I arrived at the gate, I went straight to my seat, which turned out to be an aisle seat in the very last row of economy class. Note: on most airplanes, the seats in the last row don't recline.

As I sat down, I finally got to take my first breath since Jay walked into my office and told me to head to Israel. Eventually, my heart rate had slowed down from supersonic to almost normal. Now, I had the next couple of hours to sit and think about what I forgot to do, like putting the milk back into the refrigerator before I left the house. I also needed to figure out how to explain to a certain lady friend why I wouldn't be showing up for the dinner I'd invited her to twelve hours earlier.

The flight was uneventful, with only one exception. After we ate our meals of mystery meat with Jell-O gravy, they came around to collect our trays. As I handed my tray to the flight attendant, a man seated in front of me decided to recline his seat at supersonic speed. I'm sure he forgot we were in economy class, where your knees are pressed up against the seat in front of you.

He leaned back with such force I was unable to move my legs in time and he ended up bending my toes almost straight back. I felt the pain immediately.

Not wanting to endure any more of this torture, I took the butt of my hand and with full force I punched the back of his seat. Two things immediately happened. I shattered the phone in the seat back in front of me and I launched the man's eyeglasses about three rows forward.

The man got up and gave me the evil eye. The flight attendant saw what happened and told the man that he'd hurt me when he leaned his seat back.

As I sat there with my toes throbbing for the remainder of the flight, I contemplated many different ways to get even with Jay.

Instead of the In-Flight Movie

At 5:30 a.m. I took a taxi to the train station in Osaka, Japan. When we arrived at the passenger drop-off point, the taxi in front of us stopped about 100 feet short of the designated area. My taxi driver did what comes naturally to many Asian drivers —he sounded his horn for about five seconds.

The driver in front of us must've taken exception to this because he got out of his taxi, made a fist, and swiftly pounded it into the center of the hood of our cab. My driver didn't take kindly to that, and he got out and began kicking the rear of the other driver's taxi.

I sat there and watched them scream at each other for a while, then remembered I had a train to catch. I set 1000 Yen on the driver's seat and left.

Little did I know this was only the beginning of "one of those days"...

The train ride to the airport was uneventful, but the flight from Japan to Korea was one I'll never forget. I was seated in the emergency exit row, next to another American businessman. We talked about our jobs for a while and moved on to other topics.

Meanwhile, one aisle over and about three seats back was a man who apparently started drinking long before he got on the plane at 10 a.m. Twice, he spilled his drink into the aisle. The flight attendants would clean it up, and for some silly reason, bring him another drink.

When he spilled his drink for the third time, it happened to land in the lap of an elderly man sitting across the aisle from him. The man became quite vocal and directed his anger at the drunk. Then all of a sudden, the drunk got up and started punching the elderly man.

I watched for a second and saw that nobody was going stop this, so I got up and went over to where the action was. I got there the same time as two of the flight attendants and stood there while they tried to gain control of the situation. (I didn't want to interfere with their process.)

However, when the drunk pushed one of the female flight attendants to the floor, I put the man in a bear hug, spun him around, and had him back in his seat before he could say, "I'll have another Jack Daniels, please." I stood there briefly with the flight attendants, who thanked me while they buckled him back into his seat. He was quiet for the next half hour.

Five minutes after the pilot asked the flight attendants to be seated for landing, the drunk decided it was time to take a stroll. He got up and stood in front of the in-flight map showing the current position of the plane. He just stood there and pointed at the plane on the map.

The flight attendant in front of me got up, and I followed her. Two more flight attendants were coming down the aisle from the opposite direction. They tried to put the man in his seat and he pushed one attendant hard, causing her to once again hit the floor.

Then, the man started walking toward the back of the plane. Once again, I grabbed him in a bear hug, and this time I lifted him up and carried him to a row of empty seats. I put him into a middle seat, sat in the seat beside him, and fastened his seat belt around him. The other American man came over and sat on the opposite side of him, and we both made sure he went nowhere for the remainder of the flight.

Granted, the man was drunk, which made it easy for me to maneuver him around. What I didn't understand was why nobody else was willing to help the poor flight attendants. I passed by many men who just sat there and watched like a movie was playing out in front of them.

This event took place two weeks prior to 9/11. I'm sure the responses would've been very different if it was post 9/11.

After touchdown, all of the flight attendants came by to thank me and the other American gentleman. As I was leaving the plane, one flight attendant and the captain thanked me by name (someone did some checking on me). At baggage claim, a few more people came up to me, shook my hand, and thanked me.

May I Have Your Frequent Flyer Number?

Many businesses are now utilizing interactive voice robots to take and route various types of customer support calls. Some of these robots come with a poor attempt at a pre-programmed personality, which I would guess is to make them seem more appealing.

When you join an airline's frequent flyer program, you receive certain perks, which are usually dolled out by one of these robots.

I had the "pleasure" of dealing with one of these robots while making a call from overseas with a less than adequate phone connection. The purpose of my call was to change my flight agenda. A robot with a male voice answered my call and the following conversation took place:

> Robot: Hello, and welcome. You need to state the purpose of your call. Please say, flight status, reservations, or upgrades.
>
> Me: Reservations.
>
> Robot: Thank you. Is your travel within the 50 States? Please say yes or no.
>
> Me: No.
>
> Robot: Great! Please say the name of the person who is traveling.
>
> Me: Bruce Blanton
>
> Robot: Fantastic! Okay, one last question. Please say your 11-digit frequent flyer number.
>
> Me: I say my 11-digit number.
>
> Robot: I'm sorry. I did not understand what you said. Please say your 11-digit frequent flyer number.
>
> Me: I repeated my 11-digit number.
>
> Robot: I'm sorry. I did not understand what you said. Please say your 11-digit frequent flyer number.
>
> Me: I repeated my 11-digit number (third time)
>
> Robot: I'm sorry. I did not understand what you said. Please say your 11-digit frequent flyer number.
>
> Me: I repeated my 11-digit number (fourth time)
>
> Robot: I'm sorry; I did not understand what you said. Please say your 11-digit frequent flyer number.

Me: You @#$* — #%*& — no good piece of #%$&* — stupid #$%&*! (Many words that started with the letter "F").

Robot: Got it! I will now transfer you over to an agent and I will give them the information you provided me. Thank you.

The next thing I knew, I was speaking with a live human being whose first question was, "Could you repeat your frequent flyer number for me?"

Thank you United

I'd like to use this space to say that I've spent most of my time traveling with the flight attendants and crew of United Airlines. I want to thank them for their kindness and professionalism on all of my flights. I've seen them handle everything from medical emergencies to calming down irate passengers.

My United Airlines Friends on UA 945 Frankfurt to Chicago

Only the seasoned traveler would truly understand and appreciate what flight attendants must endure as part of their jobs. I'd like to thank them for providing me with some of my most memorable experiences — of the pleasurable kind.

Not many people realize that a flight attendant's goal in life isn't to be held accountable for the taste of airplane food or to be blamed for the screaming child sitting next to you. After a long flight of babysitting people who think their needs are more important than any other passenger, these flight attendants must go home and take care of their families.

It has been a pleasure and an honor to fly with this group of people. So remember, if you're not nice to them, they'll take your picture as you drool in your sleep (complete with airplane hair) and post it on the Internet.

CRUISING

"...a 400 pound man was wearing a very small Speedo and slippers is incredibly frightening."

Expectations

If you've never cruised before, let me try to make a few things perfectly clear. First, there have been significant improvements in the cruising industry since the *Titanic* first set sail. Whenever I cruise, I usually hear at least two or three references to the *Titanic* and icebergs. It's actually pretty funny to hear first time cruisers on a Caribbean trip talk about hitting icebergs.

Actually, the biggest disaster I've had while on a cruise was the time the ship ran out of Guniess Beer and we had to wait until we got to the next island on the following day to get some more.

Next, don't base your cruising expectations on the old television series, *The Love Boat*. The ship is floating on the ocean and an old man is usually the captain — other than that, there are no similarities.

Eighty percent of your time on a ship will have something to do with either food or alcohol. If you remember watching the *Love Boat*, they always showed people sitting at a table, but they never had any food in front of them.

Finally, no matter how hard you try to avoid it, on the last night of your cruise when they slide your bar tab under your cabin door, you'll just have to accept the fact that your bar tab resembles Chicago's zip code. They never once had an episode of the *Love Boat* that had anything to do with the gigantic bar tab. (Note: if you have to open the door because your bar tab is too thick to slide under the door, you probably had a *really* good time!)

The first time you cruise, day one of being onboard will probably be filled with the word, WOW! It usually takes a day or two to get used to the experience. From the sheer size of the ship to the midnight buffet that fills a dining room the size of a small country, you'll notice that everything is over the top.

Back in my college years, there were times when I'd go out to party, fall asleep, and wake up in new surroundings. Cruising provides this same experience, but it happens in a more formal and controlled way.

It's also one of the few times where you can go out, have a good time and your "hotel" follows you home. As long as you can operate an elevator and remember your cabin number, you'll arrive home safely.

Interesting People

My first real eye opener on a cruise was when my girlfriend, Holly, and I decided to take a romantic sunset stroll on the top deck. As we walked toward the front of the ship, we encountered a vision emerging from the setting sun. We were met with a sight that still wakes me up at night in a cold sweat, and probably will continue to do so for the rest of my life.

Coming out of the sun and heading straight at us was a man who was about six feet tall and easily weighed 400 pounds. Holly and I didn't have a problem his size. However, a 400-pound man wearing a very small Speedo and slippers is incredibly frightening.

For me, the best part of taking a cruise is that you're always put into situations where you meet new people. If you're lucky, the chemistry is great and you'll form lasting friendships. This was our experience when we met two couples from Canada — David and Linda, and Dan and Margaret. Even though our homes are many miles apart, we still communicate with each other frequently and try to get together when possible to keep the friendship going.

What Time is Dinner?

When you book a cruise, there are two questions asked of you immediately. The first is, "Where are you going?" The second, "Which

Formal Night at Sea for Holly and me

dinner seating would you prefer?" Get used to it, because from that point on almost everything on your cruise will revolve around food.

At first you might not see the advantages to an early or late seating, but there are good points about both. Dinner times are usually 5:30 and 8:30. If you choose the 5:30 seating time, you must be disciplined when it comes to scheduling your day. Most of the sightseeing excursions get you back to the ship between 4 and 4:30. If that's the case, you'll have a little over an hour to look at your day's purchases and ask yourself, "Why did I just spend $50 on a wooden Jamaican mask when Wal-Mart sells them for $4.98?"

Once you get over that, you have about 45 minutes to clean up, put on your evening attire, and run to the opposite end of the ship

Time Zones, Beer & Left-Handed Chopsticks

before they close the doors to the main dining room. By the time you sit down, you're hit by total exhaustion and want to fall asleep right about the time your salad is served.

If you opt for the second seating (my preference), you'll have ample time to relax after that day's excursion. You'll have time for a pre-dinner cocktail and then a casual stroll to the dining area. Most

I wonder if this Carl's Jr in Puerto Vallarta changed their slogan to "You Can't Beat Our Meat..."

importantly, by then it will no longer bother you that you paid $50 for that dumb wooden mask.

The down side to the late seating is that you are hit with the following decision: either "pig out" now and order that second or third lobster tail, or, knowing that the midnight buffet is only two hours away from the end of dinner, decide it might be wiser to pace yourself so you have enough room for the prime rib and five layer chocolate cake at midnight.

Cabin Pressure

Another misconception the *Love Boat* leads you to believe is about the size of your cabin. On TV, the rooms look incredibly large. Unless you pay extra for a bigger room, you'll be assigned a cabin that's slightly larger than an airplane restroom.

Most people don't take cruises so they can spend a majority of time in their cabins. Most would prefer to use their cabins for sleeping and changing clothes only.

If there are two of you staying in the room and you're "lucky" enough to be assigned one of the smaller cabins, you must coordinate every movement with your partner when it comes time to get dressed. Failure to coordinate your movements will result in something that looks like a cross between professional wrestling, hide and seek, and Twister.

And ladies, a bit of advice from Holly, never take a new razor on a cruise. Keep in mind the shower area is extremely small and there's a constant sway to the boat that makes for great nicks and cuts.

Once again, it comes down to what you want to pay for your comfort. If you go the "economy route," you can get a stateroom with no windows at sea level near the engines. Or, you can pay a little more and get a room with a balcony near the top of the ship.

Once I splurged for a room with a balcony, there was no turning back. I love my space.

How Does My Cabin Stay So Clean?

On many of the cruise lines the unsung heroes are the Cabin Stewards. These are the people who use their Ninja-like skills to swoop down out of nowhere and clean your room, change your linens, laugh at that dumb mask you bought in Jamaica, and then disappear out of sight. It's almost magical the way they can restore a cabin to presentable in such a short time.

Depending on the cruise line, many of the stewards come in at night, while you are at dinner or enjoying a show, and turn down your bed. Some of them may lay out your evening or bed wear, if it's in a convenient and accessible location.

One thing that I always got a slight chuckle out of was that every night the stewards would make "Towel Critters" and leave them in special locations in our cabin. They also have classes onboard that teach you how to make these towel critters.

Excursions

Normally the cruise lines will offer lots of different activity-based excursions where you can be an active participant or just sit back and relax. You can do everything from taking a pirate ship full of rum on a tour around the bay, to feeding a stingray right out of your bare hand, or crewing on a catamaran. You might also decide to explore the "port of the day" on your own.

If you're on a Caribbean cruise and decide to wander the streets of the current port, keep in mind that many of the locals make their living off the tourists that go ashore. In the Caribbean, for example, as you go up and down the different streets you'll be asked the same questions repeatedly. If you show hesitation or don't answer immediately, the locals will walk with you and continue to question you until they get a definite response. You'll save about an hour of your time if you memorize the following phrases:

No, I don't need a taxi.

No, I don't need a mask to keep away evil spirits.

No, I don't want to take a picture with your bird.

No, I don't want to get high.

No, I don't want to see my name on a grain of rice.

I'd love to see your merchandise, but my wife has all of our money.

No, I don't want my hair braided.

There are times when a majority of the passengers leave the ship at the current port. When that happens, I often opt to stay onboard to enjoy the open space and relax.

Time Zones, Beer & Left-Handed Chopsticks

This is why friends don't let friends get their hair braided. The sign in the upper left is there for a reason.
Thanks Josh Hanson

The Rum Factory Tour

One of the ports we stopped at was in Saint Croix, where I'd signed up for The Rum Factory Tour excursion. Being the devoted researcher I am, I wanted to learn as much as I could about the trials and tribulations of the common factory worker in other countries. I wanted to know what they must endure to make a living, not to mention I wanted to see what contributions they make to society in general. In other words, I figured there would be free rum at the end of the tour.

After leaving the ship, 20 of us were taken away in mini vans. We arrived at the distillery and our tour began. We went into a barn where we were told, "This is where we make our rum." We entered the barn, climbed a ladder, and stood on an elevated walkway.

Our guide pointed to some barrels down below and simply stated, "This is where our rum is aged." We climbed down the ladder, left the barn, and entered a small room. Our guide informed us that the tour, which lasted less than ten minutes, was now complete.

We were then told that for the next hour we could either buy stuff from the gift shop or sample the various rum drinks produced at the factory. What a choice, look at jewelry made from seashells and coconuts or drink free rum. Let's just say that my decision didn't involve jewelry. After a significant number of piña coladas, our guide let us know that "happy hour" was over and we had to leave.

I was ready to go back to the ship, relax, and get rid of the slight buzz I'd acquired from consuming an assortment of local rum drinks. Unfortunately, going back to the ship wasn't next on the agenda. I was unaware that there was a "Part B" to our tour.

It was at this point that I realized I should've paid more attention to the detailed description of the excursion. I definitely want to meet the Cruise Director who decided that the logical pairing for an hour of drinking rum should be a 90-minute tour of a tropical botanical garden.

To make matters worse, it was 80/70 (80 degrees with 70% humidity). Ten minutes into our nature walk, I couldn't have cared less about which tree's sap was considered the best for making tea. I cared even less to learn that a certain purple flower made monkeys drunk.

Many of our group decided to go back to the vans and wait. Not me, I stayed with the program to learn. I learned that the *Phoenicopterus ruber rubber* (Caribbean Flamingo) eats algae, crustaceans and tiny mollusks.

This information will come in handy the next time I'm at a party or even just hanging out with the guys before a football game. I can just imagine the amazed look on the faces of my friends after I provide them with the useful information about the Caribbean Flamingo. Furthermore, they will be astonished by how I actually found a way to bring it into the conversation.

Truth told, next to standing in line at the Department of Motor Vehicles, I'd have to say the botanical garden tour was probably the longest 90 minutes of my life.

Funnel Cake

During one of our ports of call in Saint Maarten, John, Diane, Holly, and I opted to take a catamaran excursion to nearby Orient Beach. The fact that we were going to a topless beach gave John and me a "couple" of things to look forward to. These excursions are always fun because you sit on the netting at the front of the boat where you can see the ocean below and we pick up an occasional splash or two as the boat hits waves head on.

When we arrived at the beach, Holly and Diane decided to go from the catamaran to a raft and float around in the water. John and I, on the other hand, swam directly to shore because that's where the ice chest full of beer was headed.

We stood on the beach and talked with the catamaran's skipper while we depleted the contents of the ice chest. When the skipper noticed the beer inventory was almost gone, he yelled out to the catamaran to send another, then I added, "…and funnel cake!" This was a statement I would immediately regret.

No sooner had I finished saying "funnel cake," an elderly lady (born somewhere around the time Moses parted the Red Sea) came out of the water and wanted to know how we knew about funnel cake.

The regrettable part was that she was topless and between her age, old lady boobs, and the wrinkling effect of the water and the sun, she was pretty darned scary. There was no way we could un-see what we just saw. She insisted on continuing the funnel cake discussion by telling us how funnel cakes had played an important role in her youth.

Holly and Diane saw all of this taking place, but they didn't have the same perspective that John and I were forced to encounter. Eventually we caught up with our ladies back on the catamaran. They asked us about our new friend, then laughed and told us they could see our horrified expressions, even from a distance.

Questions?

When people go on a cruise, quite often they try to learn as many facts as possible about the ship and it's features. This means there are lots of questions asked of the crew, some of them quite funny. On a recent trip, the Cruise Director provided some of the questions that were asked of him by passengers:

1. Does the crew sleep on board?
2. Does the ship generate its own electricity?
3. What do you do with the ice sculptures after they melt?
4. Is the water in the toilets fresh or salt water?
5. Is this island totally surrounded by water?
6. When is the midnight buffet?

*Our Last night of a Caribbean cruise with old and new friends.
Left to right: Dan, Margaret, John, David, Diane, Linda and me.
(Holly took the picture)*

In Switzerland, I tried to meet over 50 women.
But instead, I met women over 50

LASTING MEMORIES

"…they spoke with their eyes and their hearts and that message came across very clear."

When I think of the places I've traveled, certain thoughts come to mind right away, and I'll probably never forget most of them. In some cases, you just had to be there to truly understand the emotion to appreciate what was actually happening at the moment. I'd like to share some of the many events that are special to me.

I Didn't Know His Name

I was sitting on an airplane awaiting my departure from Arizona's Sky Harbor Airport when a few people from a cancelled flight began to board. They were given instructions to sit in any open seat. A gentleman stopped and said, "Excuse me." I looked up and immediately thought I was looking at Colonel Sanders. He asked me if I'd be willing to swap my aisle seat for the open middle seat. I moved over and he sat down beside me.

Shortly after takeoff, we began some idle chat. He asked if I golfed and I told him I wanted to learn. Eventually, he got around to telling me a story about his wife. He said she always wanted to play golf with him when he was entertaining his clients. He'd never let her participate because she wasn't a very good golfer. So, while he was on his business trips, she took lessons and didn't him about it.

Patiently, she kept asking to play and was continuously denied. Finally one day, just to prove a point, he agreed to let her play. Standing at the first tee, he watched her tee up the ball and go through her warm up motions.

He was expecting to see her ball go only a few feet, but when she made contact, the ball went far and straight. He said he was speechless. She turned around, had the biggest grin on her face and a "take that" look in her eyes. Then, with the biggest smile and his eyes very wide open, he said to me, "That was a smile I'll remember 'til the day I die."

The next day at work, I was telling one of my students about this man and his story. I showed him the business card the gentleman gave me. It was then that my student told me I'd been sitting next to Karsten Solheim, founder of PING golf clubs.

Standing Tall

I was in Korea the day the World Trade Center was taken down by terrorists. The attack happened around 10 p.m. Korea time. By the time I went to work the next day, news of the tragedy was well known throughout Korea and the rest of the world.

As I stood in front of my hotel waiting for my ride to work, people passing by would stop and try to tell me how sorry they were for what had happened. Verbally, I didn't understand what any of them said, but they spoke with their eyes and their hearts and that message came across loud and clear. Their concern and compassion allowed me to stand a little bit taller while I waited. Thank you Korea!

Bless this Mess

While teaching a class in the Philippines, I was assigned to a classroom that was newly constructed on the top floor of an existing building at my customer's site. While in the middle of a lesson, the door swung open and in came five young ladies all holding lit candles. Immediately following the ladies was a priest carrying a bucket of holy water. Obviously, my discussion came to an abrupt stop.

They circled the inside of the room once, splashing holy water on everyone and everything. Then they exited the same mysterious way they'd entered. I stood there with a confused look on my face, then asked my students about what had just happened. They told me that in the Philippines, a priest must bless all new buildings. Doing this is supposed to bring good luck to the company and all people who enter it.

What Distractions?

I'd been in Korea for about a week, when one morning around 7:30 a.m., one of my students came in and looking totally exhausted. He must've been out partying the night before because everyone could smell alcohol and cigarettes long before he sat down, plus he was wearing the same clothes he'd worn the previous day.

The student came in, sat down and laid his head face down on his desk. He stayed in that position through the entire class, two breaks and one lunch hour. He didn't move. Occasionally we heard some snoring, but it was brief. Then, around 3 p.m., he made a snorting sound that actually woke him up. He sat straight up and looked around, looked at his watch, gathered his belongings, got up and left.

In the same class one day later, I was explaining an important part of how to program our machine to my four students. The door to the room opened, and a lady walked in and went over to her locker. She opened her locker and pulled out a guitar.

Without saying a word, three of my students got up, went over to the lady with the guitar and the four of them began to sing songs in Korean. Even though the music was pretty, it was not a planned portion of my class. I turned to my one remaining student and asked him to explain what had just happened. He told me that their boss was getting married in two weeks and he'd requested they play three songs at the ceremony. Apparently class time conflicted with their scheduled time for practice.

The Man in the Store Window

One night at a restaurant in Singapore, I was told I looked like Kenny Rogers. I did not take this well, because Kenny Rogers looked old to me 30 years ago. What a depressing moment, for Kenny Rogers and me. As if being told I looked like Kenny Rogers wasn't bad enough, I also had to deal with an even more ego deflating moment the very next day.

The zipper on my suitcase broke, so being the resourceful guy I am, I decided to fix it myself. I went to the large indoor shopping mall attached to the hotel where I was staying. I found a small hardware store in the center of the mall and figured it should have a pair of pliers I could buy.

While I was at the end of one aisle looking at the tools, I heard the door close. By the time I got to the door, the owner had locked it and disappeared. I'm now locked inside the hardware store.

Time Zones, Beer & Left-Handed Chopsticks

It took about five minutes of tapping on the glass door to get someone to stop and listen to me. Finally, a Japanese man and his wife stopped. I shook the door and tried to tell them I was locked in the store. They looked at me and began to laugh.

Later on, another person passing by figured out I was serious and told me he'd go get help. Ten minutes later, two shopping mall security guards arrived. They saw me standing in the store, arms folded, displaying a look of frustration. Neither of them made an attempt to communicate with me.

Apparently, one of the guards decided this was something they couldn't resolve, so he called someone on his walkie-talkie. In the meantime, the other guard grabbed the door handle and shook it, then he informed me that the door was locked. (This confirmed my opinion of mall police and showed it exists on an international level.)

Fifteen minutes had now passed and people were beginning to realize I was trapped inside the closed store. As I stood there, I noticed that I was drawing quite a crowd. They watched me for a while and then went about their business while more people showed up to watch me watch them.

Some of the people pointed at me and I figured they were telling their children something like, "That foolish man trapped in the store is the famous American singer, Kenny Rogers."

One hour and 15 minutes later, the owner came back from lunch. He was apologetic and was about as embarrassed as I was. Still remembering the original mission, I grabbed a pair of pliers. As a goodwill gesture, he gave them to me.

Power Trips

Traveling will reacquaint you with things you take for granted in everyday life, like electricity. On my first trip to Singapore, I was told I needed to get a plug adapter for my power cords. I was so intent on getting the adapter, I didn't realize there was one other question I needed to ask.

The morning after arriving in Singapore, I went to use my electric razor and discovered it had completely discharged. I got my plug adapter from my suitcase and I plugged my recharge cord into the wall via the adapter. I then plugged the other end of the cord into my razor.

As I looked at the recharge meter on the razor, it went quickly from red, to green, to orange. Just as I was thinking I had never seen it go to orange before, the razor exploded in my hands! Now when I buy products for travel, I make sure they come with a 110 to 220 volt converter.

Shortly after the Singapore trip, I was in Penang with a female coworker. I was getting ready for dinner and there was a knock on my hotel room door. When I opened the door, my coworker was standing there crying, curling iron in hand. She'd plugged her curling iron into an outlet and the increased voltage made it so hot that when she used it, it burned off a "clump" of hair. So, not only did she have a patch of missing hair, she was also giving off the distinct aroma of burnt hair.

What a Drag

One summer weekend, my girlfriend, Holly, accompanied me on one of my business trips to Portland. Holly is into flea markets, so we decided to check the paper and head out early Saturday morning to

Time Zones, Beer & Left-Handed Chopsticks

Stopping for a break while my friend Jennifer gives me a tour of Amsterdam

look for "great deals." Neither of us was familiar with the streets of Portland, so we bought some maps and were on our way.

One location in particular seemed interesting, so we decided to go there first. It was described as Oregon's biggest lakeside flea market. We drove around for a while looking for the place. Finally, from atop a bridge we saw a bunch tents down below next to the lake and figured that was where we were supposed to be. We found a place to park and started walking toward the tents.

As we were walking, we noticed some people who were dressed in a rather odd way to attend a flea market. We didn't think much of it, and figured there was another event going on somewhere close by. As we got to the area with the tents, we saw more and more oddly dressed people. We also noticed there was no merchandise in any of the booths as we walked around.

When we got to one particular booth, we were able to put everything together. We were standing in front of a booth displaying a white sign, which had lettering written with silver glitter. The sign simply read, "Spanking Booth — $2."

Both of us being of reasonable intelligence, quickly figured out that the "great deals" we were looking for were not going to be found here. It turned out that the location Holly and I actually wanted was further on down the lake. Somehow, she and I managed to wander into a location that was setting up for a Drag Queen Extravaganza and Talent Show.

Rainy Day

If you don't know the difference between a typhoon and a hurricane, don't feel too bad. It took me 42 years to figure out that there isn't a difference. Both must have winds in excess of 75 mph. The difference in their names comes from where they occur. When these storms happen in the Western Hemisphere (the Atlantic Ocean, Caribbean Sea, and Gulf of Mexico), they're hurricanes. However, if they occur in the North Pacific Ocean west of the International Date Line, they're typhoons.

One September, I got to experience the worst typhoon to hit Taiwan in 40 years. I was there to setup our booth for a semiconductor show that I'm involved with every year. After two days of setup, we were ready for the show to start the next day.

As we left the Taiwan World Trade Center, it began to rain. Later that evening, the rain started coming down hard, and the force of the wind had considerably increased. The wind and rain didn't let up for the entire night. By 6 a.m. the next morning, much of the Taipei area was severely flooded, trees were down, and highways were unusable. By 7:30 that morning, schools, businesses, and even our show had been ordered closed by the Taiwanese government.

Time Zones, Beer & Left-Handed Chopsticks

Most of the cars parked on the street in front of the hotel were beginning to fill up with the water flowing through the streets. At 9 a.m. most of Taipei was without power. To make matters worse, many of the older hotels, (including mine) kept their backup power generators in their basements, which were also flooded.

For the first few hours it was kind of amusing watching everyone gather in the lobby to comment about how hard it was raining. Watching people trying to navigate their way through the flooded streets provided some comic relief as well.

Soon the conversation turned toward how the storm had impacted everyone's reason for being in Taiwan and how much money was being lost by not starting the show as scheduled. After five hours of no power, the amusement had worn off and now everyone was becoming concerned as to when power would be restored.

With all of the inconveniences that inherently come with the loss of power, my mind seemed to be focused on only one thing — how they were going to keep the beer cold.

With most of the local businesses and restaurants closed and still no power, we were forced to have dinner at the hotel. That evening's feast was something between two slices of bread. I think it was a fish brownie. Having to eat the mystery sandwich by flashlight and wash it down with a warm soda didn't make matters any better.

Not having much else to do, I decided to just make it an early evening and go to bed.

On the second day, we were told that due to the power outage, they couldn't heat or boil water. Therefore, each room had a one-gallon box of drinking water delivered. As for showers, with no light in my bathroom and no hot water, there was no way I was going to attempt a shower, especially if I couldn't see the color of the water coming from the faucet.

Day two of the typhoon brought even more rain. After a night in a tropical climate with no air conditioning, I was starting to get pretty sticky. I decided to go down stairs to the lobby to see if there was any news regarding the restoration of power. Judging from the foul odor when I got there, it was easy for me to tell that many people were also using my "no shower" logic.

With no fresh food on hand, the hotel was resourceful enough to come up with a few cases of potato chips. The power outage was not their fault, so the hotel management saw no problem with charging us $3 for a bag of potato chips that would normally cost less than a dollar.

Since everything in the area was still closed, I had two options for the entire day. I could either hang out in the lobby with all the other non-showered people or I could go to my room and sit in total darkness. I stayed in the lobby until 7 p.m., when hunger won out over stubbornness and I decided to buy a bag of chips. I then went to my room, ate my chips, and went to bed.

Around 3 a.m., I was awakened by the power coming back on. First there was light, then the air conditioning began to function. It was like Christmas for me. I thought perhaps I should try to bathe, so I went into the bathroom and turned on the shower.

It took a few seconds before any water appeared. The first bit of water out of the faucet was yellow, and then it went orange, and then a dark brown. I let it run for about 5 minutes before deciding to just shut it off. I decided that since I had cool air, I'd just go back to bed and deal with the shower in the morning.

The next morning, I once again turned on the water for the shower. This time I discovered there was no water at all. I went down to the lobby to see what was going on. I was told the water was unsanitary and wouldn't be restored until they could flush their systems and obtain hot water.

The typhoon did its damage and left Taiwan. This meant the show could now go on. Having no way to take a real shower, I cleaned up using the remainder of my drinking water. Once I got to the World Trade Center, I saw that there were many people who hadn't cleaned up as well as I did. There were some women who definitely defined the phrase "Bad Hair Day."

At the end of the day when I returned to the hotel, it seemed to be at full operational status. At the entrance to the main elevator there was a large sign that read, "Dear customers, due to the recent typhoon the water is unsanitary. If you notice a yellow hue to the water, please do not drink it." I thought this might be useful information for people who are unsure about the proper color of tap water.

I went upstairs and took my shower in slightly yellow water, and then came back downstairs with only one issue I needed to resolve. I wanted my $3 back for that bag of chips.

Other Memorable Moments

Korea — Being taken inside the Olympic Stadium three days before the 1988 Olympics and having my picture taken as the only person in the stands.

Singapore — Sitting on the 70th floor of a hotel, looking at a beautiful sunset, drinking my very first Singapore Sling, and with a tear in my eye, enjoying the fact that I'm getting paid for this.

Philippines — After having dinner with a family of six whose entire house was no bigger than my kitchen and living room, I left their home feeling they were the lucky ones.

Ireland — Saint Patrick's Day in Dublin. Need I say more?

Japan — I asked a bartender at the hotel for directions so that I could get a late night meal. He took his apron off and drove me to the restaurant.

Taiwan — After realizing the time to get to the airport was tight, a hotel manager drove us to the airport in his personal car.

Penang — Looking at the expressions of the locals as I pulled a rickshaw up to a restaurant, with the rickshaw owner as my passenger.

Philippines — Having a surprise birthday party thrown for me by my students during class.

Israel — Kosher stir-fry.

Japan — Having a 60-year-old woman ask me to go pick grapes with her on a Sunday morning via pictures she drew.

Taiwan — Watching one of my students fight back tears as I said my good-byes after five days of classes.

Philippines — Having a taxi driver spend 45 minutes trying to explain the benefits of having the Philippines become the 51st state.

Japan — Getting into a taxi and before the driver asks where I want to go, he hands me a microphone and points to his new karaoke screen hanging from the ceiling of the cab.

Indonesia — Watching my taxi driver argue with a water buffalo because it was standing in front of his cab. He yelled, "You stupid animal, why don't you move?" I was thinking, *You have a car, why don't you drive around him?*

降り口付近では
立ち止まらないでください

Keep walking after getting off

THINK ABOUT THIS...

I have found that with all of the travel that I do, I occasionally do some things out of habit that seem strange or out of place. These actions are signs that I have been on the road too long. Here are some telling signs that you may have been away from home longer than you should.

You Know You've Traveled Too Much When...
- Your wife says "Daddy's Home" and the kids run to the telephone.
- You think you're eating authentic Mexican food in Taiwan.
- You're asked what you want for dinner and your first thought is "chairs."

- You say to yourself, "Hey, plaid pants really do go with striped shirts."
- You refer to an 11-hour flight to Japan as "short."
- You automatically dial "9" to place a call from your house.
- Immigration officials no longer laugh at your passport photo.
- Flight attendants ask you to give the preflight safety demos.
- You host a party and realize you've invited at least three taxi drivers.
- You have a favorite locker at the airport.
- You know how to replace the wheels on your luggage.
- Taxi drivers look for you.
- Bartenders in Japan send you Christmas cards.
- You say, "I saw that one on the plane" to three out of five movies.
- You make hotel reservations based on happy hour menus.
- You recognize a person you've never met, in places you've never been.
- You find it's easier to fall asleep in an airplane seat than in your own bed.
- You use your laptop monitor as your hotel room nightlight.
- You realize your hairbrush has been to more countries than most of your friends.
- You know which elevator in your hotel is the fastest.
- After waiting in baggage claim for 10 minutes, you realize you didn't check any bags.
- You try to convert the distances you've traveled in elevators into miles.

- You have deodorants from four different countries in your medicine cabinet.
- Your passport has more stamps than the number of letters you've mailed in the last year.
- You've memorized the phone number to stop the delivery of your newspaper.
- Going 80 mph on the wrong side of the road in a taxi doesn't bother you anymore.
- In Taiwan you say, "I can drive here."
- You can pack for a one-month trip in less than 10 minutes.
- You refer to your hotel room as home.
- You see your picture in travel brochures.
- You realize it's cheaper to buy new underwear than having the hotel wash them.
- Cricket scores matter to you.
- The flight attendant says, "Get it yourself; I'm busy."
- The hotel staff mistakes you for an employee.
- Vacation means staying at home.
- Corn on your pizza seems normal.
- You're afraid to get out of bed at night because you can't remember where the walls are.
- You know which hotels have the best hair dryers.
- In the Philippines, your first order of business is to find the lizard in your hotel room.
- A home cooked meal means you can read the menu.
- Every ballpoint pen in your house has a hotel name on it.
- You try to negotiate exchange rates.

- You take your suitcase in for a wheel alignment.
- When the driver no longer needs a map to return lost luggage to your house.
- You recognize rent-a-cars you've recently driven.
- In Taiwan, you look both ways before stepping on the sidewalk.
- You keep photocopied menus from restaurants in foreign countries in your briefcase.
- The hotel management asks you to be in their company picture.
- The people watching your house start having their parties in your home.
- You can tell the difference between Sumo Wrestlers.
- You come home and say things like, "When did they build that shopping mall?"
- Your travel agent asks you for advice.
- In Asia or Europe you say, "These eggs aren't that runny."
- You're not sure if you should stand in the resident or foreigner line at immigration.
- While flying you receive phone calls via the airplane telephone service.
- You hear "Window or aisle?" more times than you hear "Paper or plastic?"
- After receiving your meal in Asia, you look for the short black hair before eating.
- You can list your business address as seat 13A.
- Installing a phone in your bathroom is now a good idea.
- You can order beer in seven different languages.

Time Zones, Beer & Left-Handed Chopsticks

I guess people in Beijing needed a reminder to remain upright

Favorite Signs or Documents Translated to English

- At a bar in the Philippines: No weapons or slippers allowed.
- At a hotel in Malaysia: Notify the front desk if a body is in your room.
- At the Flying Pig Restaurant in Taiwan, the men's room had this sign: "Dear Customers, Please do not put toilet paper in the toilet.
- At a restaurant in Malaysia: You may eat your children under six for free.
- At a hotel in Japan: You must keep your clothes on while in the hallway.
- Printed on the front of a menu in a Taiwanese restaurant trying to provide Western-style eating: "Sure hope you can come."

Bruce Blanton

*Seen at a Free Clinic or under a fire extinguisher.
Meaning? You decide...*

- A sign at the entrance to an escalator in Taipei: "Please, no lay down." The text is accompanied by a stick figure of a person laying down, crossed out by a red circle and diagonal line.
- At a semiconductor company in Taiwan: You may not enter if you have AMUCKED or drank alcohol in the last 30 minutes.
- In the Taiwan guide to the city — Driver's Tips: If your parked car has disappeared, enlist the help of a Chinese-speaking friend to find it.
- On most menus, you'll find the error is just a simple misspelling. At an open-air restaurant in Bangkok, this one caught me totally off guard, "Fresh Dick Soup."
- At a semiconductor company in China: 5000 RMB ($625 USD) fine for smoking in the Fab. 500 RMB fine if you get mad or show a bad attitude when you get fined for the above or another fine.
- In China, a sign intended to indicate a handicapped men's restroom read: Deformed Man's Toilet.

- And my favorite, in a Korean hotel newspaper published for English guests, there was an article describing an Air Force plane crash: …the pilot was able to ejaculate before the plane crashed. (Personally, I would've tried to get out of the jet first.)

Points to Ponder

In Holland, everything you need under one roof!

- Are "Manila Folders" really produced in the Philippines?
- The United States is continuously looking for a solution to the problem with illegal immigrants crossing the border from Mexico. Am I the only person who recognizes that since China built their Great Wall in the 17th century, not one person from Mexico has entered China illegally?
- In Korea, you can actually take a ride on the "Seoul Train."

- On a flight to Japan, the pilot told us that we were crossing the International Dateline. I saw four people open their window shade and look out their window. What were they hoping to see?
- How many flights did it take before you realized the life jacket shown in the pre-flight demo actually looks like a yellow toilet seat cover?
- People go to many countries and refuse to drink the water, but will ask for extra ice in their soft drinks.

And Finally...

There are some people who visit another country and have their picture taken in front of a sign to get a cheap laugh. Personally, I could never do anything like that in a country where I was an invited guest just so I could get a laugh.

Thank you Gareth Edmondson

Or would I?

Thank you to Lee Sipler (right) for maintaining the sanity during many of our trips.

I would also like to thank the following people for their contributions and support:

Andy Nobuchi
Bryan Boo
Dan & Margaret Mousseau
David & Linda Potter
Gareth Edmondson
Holly Hanson
Jay Geist
Jeff Chang
Jennifer Ballentine
Josh Hanson
John and Diane Schrantz
Karen and Jeff Tunison
Lee Sipler
Rod Schwartz
Sam Nishigori
Saskia Jensen
Spencer Chung
The Lee Family (Ki, Suki, & Mikki)
Tom Crawford
Robin Surface

ABOUT THE AUTHOR

Bruce Blanton makes a living teaching people how to use computer-based products. He is sent all over the world to deliver training to his customers. Bruce is fluent in only one language, but must be able to communicate in several.

He has an exceptional ability to teach by creating pictures in a person's mind, using his friendly approach, along with imagination and humor to get his message across.

Bruce also uses his communication skills as an author to paint the same type of pictures in his readers' minds. He's not afraid to make fun of himself, especially since he quite often finds he's become the center of attention by simply trying to act normal while in unfamiliar surroundings.

You can find Bruce on Facebook at Time Zones, Beer, and Left Handed Chopsticks or go to

www.BruceBlanton.com

When you visit his website, be sure to share your travel stories.

www.ingramcontent.com/pod-product-compliance
Lightning Source LLC
Chambersburg PA
CBHW061219070526
44584CB00029B/3894